The Definitive Guide to HTML5 WebSocket

Vanessa Wang
Frank Salim
Peter Moskovits

Apress·

The Definitive Guide to HTML5 WebSocket

ISBN 978-1-4302-4740-1

ISBN 978-1-4302-4741-8 (eBook)

President and Publisher: Paul Manning
Lead Editor: Ben Renow-Clarke; Chris Nelson
Technical Reviewer: Tony Pye
Editorial Board: Steve Anglin, Mark Beckner, Ewan Buckingham, Gary Cornell, Louise Corrigan, Morgan Ertel, Jonathan Gennick, Jonathan Hassell, Robert Hutchinson, Michelle Lowman, James Markham, Matthew Moodie, Jeff Olson, Jeffrey Pepper, Douglas Pundick, Ben Renow-Clarke, Dominic Shakeshaft, Gwenan Spearing, Matt Wade, Tom Welsh
Coordinating Editor: Katie Sullivan
Copy Editor: Michael Sandlin
Compositor: SPi Global
Indexer: SPi Global
Artist: SPi Global
Cover Designer: Anna Ishchenko

Distributed to the book trade worldwide by Springer Science+Business Media New York, 233 Spring Street, 6th Floor, New York, NY 10013. Phone 1-800-SPRINGER, fax (201) 348-4505, e-mail orders-ny@springer-sbm.com, or visit www.springeronline.com. Apress Media, LLC is a California LLC and the sole member (owner) is Springer Science + Business Media Finance Inc (SSBM Finance Inc). SSBM Finance Inc is a **Delaware** corporation.

For information on translations, please e-mail rights@apress.com, or visit www.apress.com.

Apress and friends of ED books may be purchased in bulk for academic, corporate, or promotional use. eBook versions and licenses are also available for most titles. For more information, reference our Special Bulk Sales–eBook Licensing web page at www.apress.com/bulk-sales.

Any source code or other supplementary materials referenced by the author in this text is available to readers at www.apress.com. For detailed information about how to locate your book's source code, go to www.apress.com/source-code/.

To Julian, my partner in hijinks.
—Vanessa Wang

For everyone working to buid a better Web and a better world.
—Frank Salim

To Danka, Lea, and their little and not so little cousins:
Gego, Luca, Bence, Aaron, and Noah.
—Peter Moskovits

Contents at a Glance

Contents

Foreword

The browser is, hands down, the most popular and ubiquitous deployment platform available to us today: virtually every computer, smartphone, tablet, and just about every other form factor imaginable can now execute JavaScript, render a web page, and of course, talk HTTP. This, on its own, is a remarkable achievement, especially when you realize that it only took us a little over a decade to get to this stage. However, this is also just the beginning. The browser of yesterday looks nothing like what we now have access to thanks to all of the innovations of HTML5.

It is hard to overstate the importance of what HTML5 WebSocket enables: up until now, the browser could only speak one language (HTTP), and that language was not designed for the requirements of the modern, real-time Web. Yes, we've made progress with interim solutions such as long-polling and Flash sockets, but the complexity and cost of these solutions has always limited the capabilities of what we could do. WebSockets changes all of that: it is designed from the ground up to be data agnostic (binary and text), full-duplex, and optimized for minimum overhead, both in bytes and in latency.

WebSockets is TCP for the web-browser, except with a more robust and much easier to use API. Suddenly, our client is able to implement any network protocol directly in the browser, which opens up an entire new world of possibilities. An XMPP chat client? Easy. Need to connect your client to a custom binary protocol deployed on your existing network? No problem! Even better, you can script, style, and deploy these clients directly in the browser with all the web authoring tools you already know, love, and use.

The browser of yesterday talked to an HTTP server. With WebSockets, the browser can talk to anyone and implement any protocol: complete the HTTP handshake, upgrade the connection, and you are off to the races. We are no longer talking about building slightly better or more interactive pages. With WebSockets we can build entirely new types of apps and experiences that can be delivered to your users today, directly in their browser.

This book provides a great from-the-ground-up discussion of what WebSockets are, what problems they are helping us to solve, as well as a number of practical examples that will get you up and running in no time. You will be pleasantly surprised how easy it is to work with WebSocket and how much you can accomplish with very little code. Working with WebSockets is a blast, and this book by Vanessa, Frank, and Peter is a fitting guide. Enjoy!

Ilya Grigorik
Developer Advocate - Make the Web Fast, Google

About the Authors

Vanessa Wang is an HTML5 and WebSocket enthusiast who has spent more than fifteen years writing about technology. Vanessa has an MA in Education and is currently Manager of Technical Publications at Kaazing and co-organizer of the San Francisco HTML5 User Group. When she's not writing, she enjoys organizing community events for HTML5 and related technologies, kickboxing, riding her motorcycle, and playing her cello. Follow her on Twitter (@vjwang).

Frank Salim is a software engineer at Google. Previously, he was one of the original engineers at Kaazing who helped craft the WebSocket gateway and client strategy. Frank is a San Diego native currently residing in San Francisco, California. He holds a degree in computer science from Pomona College. When he is not programming, Frank enjoys reading, painting, and inline skating. In 2010, Frank co-authored *Pro HTML5 Programming* (Apress).

Peter Moskovits is the head of real-time solutions development at Kaazing, a software company enhancing the way businesses and customers communicate across the Web using the new HTML5 WebSocket standard. Peter works closely with architects and the developer community to build and deploy the best possible web communication solutions. Before joining Kaazing, Peter held various product management leadership roles and was responsible for Oracle's portal product strategy. Peter is a frequent speaker at conferences and industry events, such as GoTo, YOW!, JavaOne, Oracle OpenWorld, HTML5DeConf, DevCon5, and various user group meetings. He is also the co-author of the *Oracle WebCenter 11g Handbook.*

About the Technical Reviewer

 **Tony Pye** has a background in software consultancy, web development, and engineering. However, instead of taking his technical expertise into manufacturing, he took the path to geekdom and in 2003 became a partner and head of digital production at INK Digital Agency, one of the UK's national Top 10 digital agencies.*

In addition to having an extensive knowledge of current software and coding standards, Tony keeps a sharp eye on the future, watching for emerging technologies, thus ensuring his team remains at the forefront of an ever-changing digital landscape. Although businesses face many challenges, Tony has the underlying knowledge and experience to define their technical problems and produce innovative digital solutions for a range of commercial environments.

In his spare time, Tony particularly enjoys traveling to sunnier climes where he can pursue his passion for scuba diving. You can contact Tony via email at tony@inkdigitalagency.com.

---

*Nominated in the Recommended Agency Register (RAR) awards 2012.

Acknowledgments

Many thanks to Peter Lubbers (*Pro HTML5 Programming, 2nd ed.*), whose guidance and enthusiasm for HTML5 made this book possible, and to Ilya Grigorik whose passion for web performance and real-time technologies is truly inspiring. Thanks to Steve Atkinson and Frank Greco, who tirelessly provided insightful feedback at odd hours of the day and night. Much gratitude to Jeff Mesnil and Dhurv Matani for their awesome code (check them out on GitHub!) that enabled some of the cutting-edge examples we used in this book. Special thanks to Kaazing and Apress for their support and giving us the opportunity to share our passion for WebSocket.

Vanessa Wang
Frank Salim
Peter Moskovits

My deepest appreciation to Julian for his encouragement, support, and never-ending patience. Thanks to Camper and Tilson for simply being awesome, and to the Pins for not-so-silently keeping me company during the late nights and early mornings. Special thanks to my family for all the sacrifices they made to put me here.

And, finally, much gratitude and respect to my incredible co-authors and friends, Frank and Peter, for their brilliance, creativity, and enthusiasm.

Vanessa Wang

I'd like to sincerely thank my family for their support, having thanked them more facetiously in the past. I would like to thank April for her excellent advice and patience. Of course, I would also like to thank my co-authors, Vanessa and Peter.

Frank Salim

Thank you, Anna, for your incredible support and understanding while working on the book . . . and beyond. I'm thankful to Danka and Lea, the sweetest kids ever, who were so easy on me and didn't (always) get upset when I had to sit down and work. Special thanks to Aniko for her tireless help.

And last, but not least, I'm grateful that I could work with my two co-authors, Vanessa and Frank, two exceptional colleagues and friends. Thank you guys for the opportunity - I enjoyed every moment of it.

Peter Moskovits

CHAPTER 1

Introduction to HTML5 WebSocket

This book is for anyone who wants to learn how to build real-time web applications. You might say to yourself, "I already do that!" or ask "What does that really mean?" Let's clarify: this book will show you how to build *truly* real-time web applications using a revolutionary new and widely supported open industry standard technology called WebSocket, which enables full-duplex, bidirectional communication between your client application and remote servers over the Web—without plugins!

Still confused? So were we a few years ago, before we started working with HTML5 WebSocket. In this guide, we'll explain what you need to know about WebSocket, and why you should be thinking about using WebSocket today. We will show you how to implement a WebSocket client in your web application, create your own WebSocket server, use WebSocket with higher-level protocols like XMPP and STOMP, secure traffic between your client and server, and deploy your WebSocket-based applications. Finally, we will explain why you should be thinking about using WebSocket right now.

What is HTML5?

First, let's examine the "HTML5" part of "HTML5 WebSocket." If you're already an expert with HTML5, having read, say, *Pro HTML5 Programming*, and are already developing wonderfully modern and responsive web applications, then feel free to skip this section and read on. But, if you're new to HTML5, here's a quick introduction.

HTML was originally designed for static, text-based document sharing on the Internet. Over time, as web users and designers wanted more interactivity in their HTML documents, they began enhancing these documents, by adding form functionality and early "portal" type capabilities. Now, these static document collections, or web sites, are more like web *applications*, based on the principles of rich client/server desktop applications. These web applications are being used on almost any device: laptops, smart phones, tablets—the gamut.

HTML5 is designed to make the development of these rich web applications easier, more natural, and more logical, where developers can design and build once, and deploy anywhere. HTML5 makes web applications more usable, as well, as it removes the need for plugins. With HTML5, you now use semantic markup language like <header> instead of <div class="header">. Multimedia is also much easier to code, by using tags like

`<audio>` and `<video>` to pull in and assign the appropriate media type. Additionally, by being semantic, HTML5 is more accessible, since screen readers can more easily read its tags.

HTML5 is an umbrella term that covers the large number of improvements and changes happening in web technologies, and includes everything from the markup you use on your web pages to the CSS3 styling, offline and storage, multimedia, connectivity, and so on. Figure 1-1 shows the different HTML5 feature areas.

Figure 1-1. *HTML5 feature areas (W3C, 2011)*

There are lots of resources that delve into these areas of HTML5. In this book, we focus on the Connectivity area, namely the WebSocket API and protocol. Let's take a look at the history of HTML5 connectivity.

HTML5 Connectivity

The Connectivity area of HTML5 includes technologies like WebSocket, Server-Sent Events, and Cross-Document Messaging. These APIs were included in the HTML5 specification to help simplify some of the areas where browser limitations prevented web application developers from creating the rich behavior they desired or where web application development was becoming overly complex. One example of simplification in HTML5 is Cross-Document Messaging.

Before HTML5, communication between browser windows and frames was restricted for security reasons. However, as web applications started to bring together content and applications from different web sites, it became necessary for those applications to communicate with each other. To address this, standards bodies and major browser vendors agreed to support Cross-Document Messaging, which enables secure cross-origin communication across browser windows, tabs, and iFrames. Cross-Document Messaging defines the postMessage API as a standard way to send and receive messages. There are many use cases for consuming content from different hosts and domains—such as mapping, chat, and social networks—to communicate inside the web browser. Cross-Document Messaging provides asynchronous messages passing between JavaScript contexts.

The HTML5 specification for Cross-Document Messaging also clarifies and refines domain security by introducing the concept of *origin*, which is defined by a scheme, host, and port. Basically, two URIs are considered from the same origin if and only if they have the *same scheme, host and port*. The path is not considered in the origin value.

The following examples show mismatched schemes, hosts, and ports (and therefore different origins):

- **https://**www.example.com and **http://**www.example.com

- http://**www.example.com** and http://**example.com**

- http://example.com:**8080** and http://example.com:**8081**

The following examples are URLs of the same origin:
http://www.example.com/page1.html and http://www.example.com/page2.html.

Cross-Document Messaging overcomes the same-origin limitation by allowing messages to be exchanged between different origins. When you send a message, the sender specifies the receiver's origin and when you receive a message the sender's origin is included as part of the message. The origin of the message is provided by the browser and cannot be spoofed. On the receiver's side, you can decide which messages to process and which to ignore. You can also keep a "white list" and process only messages from documents with trusted origins.

Cross-Document Messaging is a great example of where the HTML5 specification simplifies communication between web applications with a very powerful API. However, its focus is limited to communicating across windows, tabs, and iFrames. It does not address the complexities that have become overwhelming in protocol communication, which brings us to WebSocket.

Ian Hickson, the lead writer of the HTML5 specification, added what we now call WebSocket to the Communication section of the HTML5 specification. Originally called TCPConnection, WebSocket has evolved into its own independent specification. While WebSocket now lives outside the realm of HTML5, it's important for achieving real-time connectivity in modern (HTML5-based) web applications. WebSocket is also often discussed as part of the Connectivity area of HTML5. So, why is WebSocket meaningful in today's Web? Let's first take a look at older HTTP architectures where protocol communication is significant.

Overview of Older HTTP Architectures

To understand the significance of WebSocket, let's first take a look at older architectures, specifically those that use HTTP.

HTTP 101 (or rather, HTTP/1.0 and HTTP/1.1)

In older architectures, connectivity was handled by HTTP/1.0 and HTTP/1.1. HTTP is a protocol for request-response in a client/server model, where the client (typically a web browser) submits an HTTP request to the server, and the server responds with the requested resources, such as an HTML page, as well as additional information about the page. HTTP was also designed for fetching documents; HTTP/1.0 sufficed for a single document request from a server. However, as the Web grew beyond simple document sharing and began to include more interactivity, connectivity needed to be refined to enable quicker response time between the browser request and the server response.

In HTTP/1.0, a separate connection was made for *every* request to the server, which, to say the least, did not scale well. The next revision of HTTP, HTTP/1.1, added reusable connections. With the introduction of reusable connections, browsers could initialize a connection to a web server to retrieve the HTML page, then reuse the same connection to retrieve resources like images, scripts, and so on. HTTP/1.1 reduced latency between requests by reducing the number of connections that had to be made from clients to servers.

HTTP is stateless, which means it treats each request as unique and independent. There are advantages to a stateless protocol: for example, the server doesn't need to keep information about the session and thus doesn't require storage of that data. However, this also means that redundant information about the request is sent for every HTTP request and response.

Let's take a look at an example HTTP/1.1 request from a client to a server. Listing 1-1 shows a complete HTTP request containing several HTTP headers.

Listing 1-1. HTTP/1.1 Request Headers from the Client to the Server

```
GET /PollingStock/PollingStock HTTP/1.1
Host: localhost:8080
User-Agent: Mozilla/5.0 (Windows; U; Windows NT 5.1; en-US; rv:1.9.1.5)
Gecko/20091102 Firefox/3.5.5
Accept: text/html,application/xhtml+xml,application/xml;q=0.9,*/*;q=0.8
Accept-Language: en-us
Accept-Encoding: gzip,deflate
Accept-Charset: ISO-8859-1,utf-8;q=0.7,*;q=0.7
Keep-Alive: 300
Connection: keep-alive
Referer: http://localhost:8080/PollingStock/
Cookie: showInheritedConstant=false; showInheritedProtectedConst
ant=false; showInheritedProperty=false; showInheritedProtectedPr
operty=false; showInheritedMethod=false; showInheritedProtectedM
ethod=false; showInheritedEvent=false; showInheritedStyle=false;
showInheritedEffect=false;
```

Listing 1-2 shows an example HTTP/1.1 response from a server to a client.

Listing 1-2. HTTP/1.1 Response Headers from the Server to the Client

```
HTTP/1.x 200 OK
X-Powered-By: Servlet/2.5
Server: Sun Java System Application Server 9.1_02
Content-Type: text/html;charset=UTF-8
Content-Length: 321
Date: Wed, 06 Dec 2012 00:32:46 GMT
```

In Listings 1-1 and 1-2, the total overhead is 871 bytes of solely header information (that is, no actual data). These two examples show just the request's header information that goes over the wire in each direction: from the client to the server, and the server to client, regardless of whether the server has actual data or information to deliver to the client.

With HTTP/1.0 and HTTP/1.1, the main inefficiencies stem from the following:

- HTTP was designed for document sharing, not the rich, interactive applications we've become accustomed to on our desktops and now the Web

- The amount of information that the HTTP protocol requires to communicate between the client and server adds up quickly the more interaction you have between the client and server

By nature, HTTP is also *half duplex*, meaning that traffic flows in a single direction at a time: the client sends a request to the server (one direction); the server then responds to the request (one direction). Being half duplex is simply inefficient. Imagine a phone conversation where every time you want to communicate, you must press a button, state your message, and press another button to complete it. Meanwhile, your conversation partner must patiently wait for you to finish, press the button, and then finally respond in kind. Sound familiar? We used this form of communication as kids on a small scale, and our military uses this all the time: it's a walkie-talkie. While there are definitely benefits and great uses for walkie-talkies, they are not always the most efficient form of communication.

Engineers have been working around this issue for years with a variety of well-known methods: polling, long polling, and HTTP streaming.

The Long Way Around: HTTP Polling, Long Polling, and Streaming

Normally when a browser visits a web page, an HTTP request is sent to the server that hosts that page. The web server acknowledges the request and sends the response back to the web browser. In many cases, the information being returned, such as stock prices, news, traffic patterns, medical device readings, and weather information, can be stale by the time the browser renders the page. If your users need to get the most up-to-date real-time information, they can constantly manually refresh the page, but that's obviously an impractical and not a particularly elegant solution.

Current attempts to provide real-time web applications largely revolve around a technique called *polling* to simulate other server-side push technologies, the most popular of which is *Comet*, which basically delays the completion of an HTTP response to deliver messages to the client.

Polling is a regularly timed synchronous call where the client makes a request to the server to see if there's any information available for it. The requests are made at regular intervals; the client receives a response, regardless of whether there's information. Specifically, if there's information available, the server sends it. If no information is available, the server returns a negative response and the client closes the connection.

Polling is a good solution if you know the exact interval of message delivery, because you can synchronize the client to send a request only when you know information will be available on the server. However, real-time data is often not that predictable, and making unnecessary requests and therefore superfluous connections is inevitable. Consequently, you may open and close many connections needlessly in a low-message rate situation.

Long polling is another popular communication method, where the client requests information from the server and opens a connection during a set time period. If the server does not have any information, it holds the request open until it has information for the client, or until it reaches the end of a designated timeout. At that point, the client re-requests the information from the server. Long polling is also known as Comet, which we mentioned earlier, or Reverse AJAX. Comet delays the completion of the HTTP response until the server has something to send to the client, a technique often called a hanging-GET or pending-POST. It's important to understand that when you have a high message volume, long polling does not provide significant performance improvements over traditional polling, because the client must constantly reconnect to the sever to fetch new information, resulting in the network behavior equivalent to rapid polling. Another issue with long polling is the lack of standard implementations.

With *streaming*, the client sends a request, and the server sends and maintains an open response that is continually updated and kept open (either indefinitely or for a set period of time). The server updates the response whenever a message is ready to be delivered. While streaming sounds like a great solution to accommodate unpredictable message delivery, the server never signals to complete the HTTP response, and thus the connection remains open continuously. In such situations, proxies and firewalls may buffer the response, resulting in increased latency of the message delivery. Therefore, many streaming attempts are brittle on networks where firewalls or proxies are present.

These methods provide almost-real-time communication, but they also involve HTTP request and response headers, which contain lots of additional and unnecessary header data and latency. Additionally, in each case, the client must wait for requests to return before it can initiate subsequent requests, therefore significantly increasing latency.

Figure 1-2 shows the half duplex nature of these connections over the Web, integrating into an architecture where you have full duplex connections over TCP in your intranet.

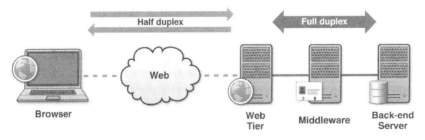

Figure 1-2. *Half duplex over the Web; Full duplex over TCP on the back-end*

Introducing WebSocket

So, where does this bring us? To eliminate many of these issues, the Connectivity section of the HTML5 specification includes WebSocket. WebSocket is a naturally full-duplex, bidirectional, single-socket connection. With WebSocket, your HTTP request becomes a single request to open a WebSocket connection (either WebSocket or WebSocket over TLS (Transport Layer Security, formerly known as SSL)), and reuses the same connection from the client to the server, and the server to the client.

WebSocket reduces latency because once the WebSocket connection is established, the server can send messages as they become available. For example, unlike polling, WebSocket makes a single request. The server does not need to wait for a request from the client. Similarly, the client can send messages to the server at any time. This single request greatly reduces latency over polling, which sends a request at intervals, regardless of whether messages are available.

Figure 1-3 compares a sample polling scenario with a WebSocket scenario.

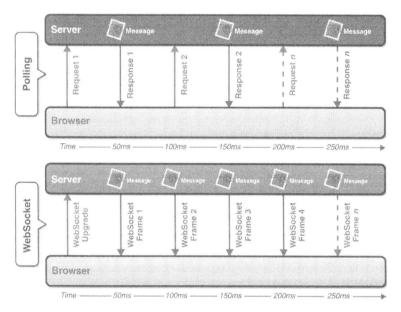

Figure 1-3. *Polling vs WebSocket*

In essence, WebSocket fits into the HTML5 paradigm of semantics and simplification. It not only eliminates the need for complicated workarounds and latency but also simplifies the architecture. Let's delve into the reasons a bit further.

Why Do You Need WebSocket?

Now that we've explored the history that brought us to WebSocket, let's look at some of the reasons why you *should* use WebSocket.

WebSocket is about *Performance*

WebSocket makes real-time communication much more efficient.

You can always use polling (and sometimes even streaming) over HTTP to receive notifications over HTTP. However, WebSocket saves bandwidth, CPU power, and latency.

WebSocket is an innovation in performance.

WebSocket is about *Simplicity*

WebSocket makes communication between a client and server over the Web much simpler.

Those who have already gone through the headache of establishing real-time communication in pre-WebSocket architectures know that techniques for real-time notification over HTTP are overly complicated. Maintaining session state across stateless requests adds complexity. Cross-origin AJAX is convoluted, processing ordered requests with AJAX requires special consideration, and communicating with AJAX is complicated. Every attempt to stretch HTTP into use cases for which it was not designed increases software complexity.

WebSocket enables you to dramatically simplify connection-oriented communication in real-time applications.

WebSocket is about *Standards*

WebSocket is an underlying network protocol that enables you to build other standard protocols on top of it.

Many web applications are essentially monolithic. Most AJAX applications typically consist of tightly coupled client and server components. Because WebSocket naturally supports the concept of higher-level application protocols, you can more flexibly evolve clients and servers independently of one another. Supporting these higher-level protocols enables modularity and encourages the development of reusable components. For example, you can use the same XMPP over WebSocket client to sign in to different chat servers because all XMPP servers understand the same standard protocol.

WebSocket is an innovation in interoperable web applications.

WebSocket is about *HTML5*

WebSocket is part of an effort to provide advanced capabilities to HTML5 applications in order to compete with other platforms.

Every operating system needs networking capabilities. The ability for applications to open sockets and communicate with other hosts is a core feature provided by every major platform. HTML5 is, in many ways, a trend toward making web browsers fully capable application platforms that are analogous to operating systems. Low-level networking APIs like sockets would not mesh with the origin security model or API design style of the Web. WebSocket provides TCP-style networking for HTML5 applications without wrecking browser security *and* it has a modern API.

WebSocket is a key component of the HTML5 platform and an incredibly powerful tool for developers.

You Need WebSocket!

Simply put, you need WebSocket to build world-class web applications. WebSocket addresses the major deficiencies that make HTTP unsuitable for real-time communication. The asynchronous, bidirectional communication patterns enabled by WebSocket are a return to the general flexibility afforded by transport layer protocols on the Internet.

Think about all the great ways you can use WebSocket and build true real-time functionality into your applications, like chat, collaborative document editing, massively multiplayer online (MMO) games, stock trading applications, and the list goes on. We'll take a look at specific applications later in this book.

WebSocket and RFC 6455

WebSocket is a protocol, but there is also a WebSocket API, which enables your applications to control the WebSocket protocol and respond to events triggered by the server. The API is developed by the W3C (World Wide Web Consortium) and the protocol by the IETF (Internet Engineering Task Force). The WebSocket API is now supported by modern browsers and includes methods and attributes needed to use a full duplex, bidirectional WebSocket connection. The API enables you to perform necessary actions like opening and closing the connection, sending and receiving messages, and listening for events triggered by the server. Chapter 2 describes the API in more detail and gives examples of how to use the API.

The WebSocket Protocol enables full duplex communication between a client and a remote server over the Web, and supports transmission of binary data and text strings. The protocol consists of an opening handshake followed by basic message framing, and is layered over TCP. Chapter 3 describes the protocol in more detail and shows you how to create your own WebSocket server.

The World of WebSocket

The WebSocket API and protocol have a thriving community, which is reflected by a variety of WebSocket server options, developer communities, and myriad real-life WebSocket applications that are being used today.

WebSocket Options

There are a variety of WebSocket server implementations available out there, such as Apache mod_pywebsocket, Jetty, Socket.IO, and Kaazing's WebSocket Gateway.

The idea for *The Definitive Guide for HTML5 WebSocket* was born from the desire to share our knowledge, experiences, and opinions from years of working with WebSocket and related technologies at Kaazing. Kaazing has been building an enterprise WebSocket gateway server and its client libraries for over five years.

The WebSocket Community: It Lives!

We've listed a few reasons to use WebSocket and will explore real, applicable examples of how you can implement WebSocket yourself. In addition to the wide variety of WebSocket servers available, the WebSocket community is thriving, especially regarding HTML5 gaming, enterprise messaging, and online chat. Every day, there are more conferences and coding sessions devoted not only to specific areas of HTML5 but also to real-time communication methods, especially WebSocket. Even companies that build widely used enterprise messaging services are integrating WebSocket into their systems. Because WebSocket is standards-based, it's easy to enhance your existing architecture, standardize and extend your implementations, as well as build new services that were previously impossible or difficult to build.

The excitement around WebSocket is also reflected in online communities like GitHub, where more WebSocket-related servers, applications, and projects are created daily. Other online communities that are thriving are `http://www.websocket.org`, which hosts a WebSocket server we will use as an example in the subsequent chapters and `http://webplatform.org` and `http://html5rocks.com`, which are open communities that encourage the sharing of all information related to HTML5, including WebSocket.

▓ **Note**   More WebSocket servers are listed in Appendix B.

Applications of WebSocket

At the time of writing this book, WebSocket is being used for a wide variety of applications. Some applications were possible with previous "real-time" communication technologies like AJAX, but they have dramatically increased performance. Foreign exchange and stock quote applications have also benefited from the reduced bandwidth and full-duplex connection that WebSocket provides. We'll take a look at how you can examine WebSocket traffic in Chapter 3.

With the increase in application deployment to the browser, there has also been a boom to HTML5 games development. WebSocket is a natural fit for gaming over the Web, as gameplay and game interaction are incredibly reliant on responsiveness. Some examples of HTML5 games that use WebSocket are popular online betting applications, game controller applications that integrate with WebGL over WebSocket, and in-game online chat. There are also some very exciting massively multiplayer online (MMO) games that are widely used in browsers from all types of mobile and desktop devices.

Related Technologies

You may be surprised to learn that there are other technologies that you can use in conjunction with or as an alternative to WebSocket. The following are a few other emerging web communication technologies.

Server-Sent Events

WebSocket is a good choice for when your architecture requires bidirectional, full duplex communication. However, if your service primarily broadcasts or pushes information to its clients and does not require any interactivity (such as newsfeeds, weather forecasts, and so on), then using the EventSource API provided by Server-Sent Events (SSE) is a good option. SSE, which is part of the HTML5 specification, consolidates some Comet techniques. It is possible to use SSE as a common, interoperable syntax for HTTP polling, long polling, and streaming. With SSE, you get auto-reconnect, event IDs, and so on.

▓ **Note**   Although WebSocket and SSE connections both begin with HTTP requests, the performance benefits you see and their abilities might be quite different. For example, SSE cannot send streaming data upstream from the client to the server and supports only text data.

SPDY

SPDY (pronounced "speedy") is a networking protocol being developed by Google, and is supported by a growing number of browsers, including Google Chrome, Opera, and Mozilla Firefox. In essence, SPDY augments HTTP to improve the performance of HTTP requests by doing things like compressing HTTP headers and multiplexing. Its main purpose is to improve the performance of web *pages*. While WebSocket is focused on optimizing communication between web application front-ends and servers, SPDY optimizes delivery application content and static pages, as well. The differences between HTTP and WebSocket are architectural, not incremental. SPDY is a revised form of HTTP, so it shares the same architectural style and semantics. It fixes many of the non-intrinsic problems with HTTP, adding multiplexing, working pipelining, and other useful enhancements. WebSocket removes request-response style communication and enables real-time interaction and alternative architectural patterns.

WebSocket and SPDY are complementary; you will be able to upgrade your SPDY-augmented HTTP connection to WebSocket, thus using WebSocket over SPDY and benefitting from the best of both worlds.

Web Real-Time Communication

Web Real-Time Communication (WebRTC) is another effort to enhance the communication capabilities of modern web browsers. WebRTC is peer-to-peer technology for the Web. Browsers can communicate directly without funneling all of the data through a server. WebRTC includes APIs that let browsers communicate with each other in real time. At the time of writing this book, the WebRTC is still in draft format by the World Wide Web Consortium (W3C) and can be found at http://www.w3.org/TR/webrtc/.

The first applications for WebRTC are real-time voice and video chat. WebRTC is already a compelling new technology for media applications, and there are many available sample applications online that enable you to test this out with video and audio over the Web.

WebRTC will later add data channels. These data channels are planned to use similar API as WebSocket for consistency. Additionally, if your application makes use of streaming media and other data, you can use both WebSocket and WebRTC together.

Summary

In this chapter, you were introduced to HTML5 and WebSocket and learned a little bit about the history of HTTP that brought us to WebSocket. We hope that by now you're as excited as we are to learn more about WebSocket, get into the code, and dream about all the wonderful things you'll be able to do with it.

In the subsequent chapters, we'll delve more into the WebSocket API and protocol and explain how to use WebSocket with standard, higher-level application protocols, talk about security aspects of WebSocket, and describe enterprise-level features and deployment.

CHAPTER 2

■ ■ ■

The WebSocket API

This chapter introduces you to the WebSocket Application Programming Interface (API), which you can use to control the WebSocket Protocol and create WebSocket applications. In this chapter, we examine the building blocks of the WebSocket API, including its events, methods, and attributes. To learn how to use the API, we write a simple client application, connect to an existing, publicly available server (http://websocket.org), which allows us to send and receive messages over WebSocket. By using an existing server, we can focus on learning about the easy-to-use API that enables you to create WebSocket applications. We also explain step-by-step how to use the WebSocket API to power HTML5 media using binary data. Finally, we discuss browser support and connectivity.

This chapter focuses on the client application side of WebSocket, which enables you to extend the WebSocket Protocol to your web applications. The subsequent chapters will describe the WebSocket Protocol itself, as well as using WebSocket within your environment.

Overview of the WebSocket API

As we mentioned in Chapter 1, WebSocket consists of the network protocol and an API that enable you to establish a WebSocket connection between a client application and the server. We will discuss the protocol in greater detail in Chapter 3, but let's first take a look at the API.

The WebSocket API is an interface that enables applications to use the WebSocket Protocol. By using the API with your applications, you can control a full-duplex communication channel through which your application can send and receive messages. The WebSocket interface is very straightforward and easy to use. To connect to a remote host, you simply create a new WebSocket object instance and provide the new object with a URL that represents the endpoint to which you wish to connect.

A WebSocket connection is established by upgrading from the HTTP protocol to the WebSocket Protocol during the initial handshake between the client and the server, over the same underlying TCP connection. Once established, WebSocket messages can be sent back and forth between the methods defined by the WebSocket interface. In your application code, you then use asynchronous event listeners to handle each phase of the connection life cycle.

The WebSocket API is purely (and truly) event driven. Once the full-duplex connection is established, when the server has data to send to the client, or if resources that you care about change their state, it automatically sends the data or notifications.

With an event-driven API, you do not need to poll the server for the most updated status of the targeted resource; rather, the client simply listens for desired notifications and changes.

We will see different examples of using the WebSocket API in the subsequent chapters when we talk about higher-level protocols, such as STOMP and XMPP. For now, though, let's take a closer look at the API.

Getting Started with the WebSocket API

The WebSocket API enables you to establish full-duplex, bidirectional communication over the Web between your client application and server-side processes. The WebSocket interface specifies the methods that are available for the client and how the client interacts with the network.

To get started, you first create a WebSocket connection by calling the WebSocket constructor. The constructor returns a WebSocket object instance. You can listen for events on that object. These events tell you when the connection opens, when messages arrive, when the connection closes, and when errors occur. You can interact with the WebSocket instance to send messages or close the connection. The subsequent sections explore each of these aspects of the WebSocket API.

The WebSocket Constructor

To establish a WebSocket connection to a server, you use the WebSocket interface to instantiate a WebSocket object by pointing to a URL that represents the endpoint to which you want to connect. The WebSocket Protocol defines two URI schemes, ws and wss for unencrypted and encrypted traffic between the client and the server, respectively. The ws (WebSocket) scheme is analogous to an HTTP URI scheme. The wss (WebSocket Secure) URI scheme represents a WebSocket connection over Transport Layer Security (TLS, also known as SSL), and uses the same security mechanism that HTTPS uses to secure HTTP connections.

■ **Note**   We'll discuss WebSocket security in depth in Chapter 7.

The WebSocket constructor takes one required argument, URL (the URL to which you want to connect) and one optional argument, protocols (either a single protocol name or an array of protocol names that the server must include in its response to establish the connection). Examples of protocols you can use in the protocols argument are XMPP (Extensible Messaging and Presence Protocol), SOAP (Simple Object Access Protocol), or a custom protocol.

Listing 2-1 illustrates the one required argument in the WebSocket constructor, which must be a fully qualified URL starting with the ws:// or wss:// scheme. In this example, the fully qualified URL is ws://www.websocket.org. If there is a syntax error in the URL, the constructor will throw an exception.

Listing 2-1. Sample WebSocket Constructor

```
// Create new WebSocket connection

var ws = new WebSocket("ws://www.websocket.org");
```

When connecting to a WebSocket server, you can optionally use the second argument to list the protocols your application supports, namely for protocol negotiation.

To ensure that the client and the server are sending and receiving messages they both understand, they must use the same protocol. The WebSocket constructor enables you to define the protocol or protocols that your client can use to communicate with a server. The server in turn selects the protocol to use; only one protocol can be used between a client and a server. These protocols are used over the WebSocket Protocol. One of the great benefits of WebSocket, as you'll learn in Chapters 3 through 6, is the ability to layer widely used protocols over WebSocket, which lets you do great things like take traditional desktop applications to the Web.

▨ **Note** The WebSocket Protocol (RFC 6455) refers to protocols you can use with WebSocket as "subprotocols," even though they are higher-level, fully formed protocols. Throughout this book, we'll generally refer to protocols that you can use with WebSocket simply as "protocols" to avoid confusion.

Before we get too far ahead of ourselves, let's return to the WebSocket constructor in the API. During the initial WebSocket connection handshake, which you'll learn more about in Chapter 3, the client sends a `Sec-WebSocket-Protocol` header with the protocol name. The server chooses zero or one protocol and responds with a `Sec-WebSocket-Protocol` header with the same name the client requested; otherwise, it closes the connection.

Protocol negotiation is useful for determining which protocol or version of a protocol a given WebSocket server supports. An application might support multiple protocols and use protocol negotiation to select which protocol to use with a particular server. Listing 2-2 shows the WebSocket constructor with support for a hypothetical protocol, "myProtocol":

Listing 2-2. Sample WebSocket Constructor with Protocol Support

```
// Connecting to the server with one protocol called myProtocol

var ws = new WebSocket("ws://echo.websocket.org", "myProtocol");
```

▨ **Note** In Listing 2-2, the hypothetical protocol "myProtocol" is a well-defined, perhaps even registered and standardized, protocol name that both the client application and the server can understand.

The WebSocket constructor can also include an array of protocol names that the client supports, which lets the server decide which one to use. Listing 2-3 shows a sample WebSocket constructor with a list of protocols it supports, represented as an array:

Listing 2-3. Sample WebSocket Constructor with Protocol Support

```
// Connecting to the server with multiple protocol choices

var echoSocket = new
WebSocket("ws://echo.websocket.org", ["com.kaazing.echo",
"example.imaginary.protocol"])

echoSocket.onopen = function(e) {
    // Check the protocol chosen by the server
    console.log(echoSocket.protocol);
}
```

In Listing 2-3, because the WebSocket server at ws://echo.websocket.org only understands the com.kaazing.echo protocol and not example.imaginary.protocol, the server chooses the com.kaazing.echo protocol when the WebSocket open event fires. Using an array gives you flexibility in enabling your application to use different protocols with different servers.

We'll discuss the WebSocket Protocol in depth in the next chapter, but in essence, there are three types of protocols you can indicate with the protocols argument:

- Registered protocols: Standard protocols that have been officially registered according to RFC 6455 (The WebSocket Protocol) and with the IANA (Internet Assigned Numbers Authority), the official governing body for registered protocols. An example of a registered protocol is Microsoft's SOAP over WebSocket protocol. See http://www.iana.org/assignments/websocket/websocket.xml for more information.

- Open protocols: Widely used and standardized protocols like XMPP and STOMP, which have not been registered as official standard protocols. We will examine how to use these types of protocols with WebSocket in the subsequent chapters.

- Custom protocols: Protocols that you've written and want to use with WebSocket.

In this chapter, we focus on using the WebSocket API as you would for your own custom protocol and examine using open protocols in the later chapters. Let's take a look at the events, objects, and methods individually and put them together into a working example.

WebSocket Events

The WebSocket API is purely event driven. Your application code listens for events on WebSocket objects in order to handle incoming data and changes in connection status. The WebSocket Protocol is also event driven. Your client application does not need to poll the server for updated data. Messages and events will arrive asynchronously as the server sends them.

WebSocket programming follows an asynchronous programming model, which means that as long as a WebSocket connection is open, your application simply listens for events. Your client does not need to actively poll the server for more information. To start listening for the events, you simply add callback functions to the WebSocket object. Alternatively, you can use the addEventListener() DOM method to add event listeners to your WebSocket objects.

A WebSocket object dispatches four different events:

- Open
- Message
- Error
- Close

As with all web APIs, you can listen for these events using on<eventname> handler properties, as well as using the addEventListener(); method.

WebSocket Event: Open

Once the server responds to the WebSocket connection request, the open event fires and a connection is established. The corresponding callback to the open event is called onopen.

Listing 2-4 illustrates how to handle the event when the WebSocket connection is established.

Listing 2-4. Sample Open Event Handler

```
// Event handler for the WebSocket connection opening
ws.onopen = function(e) {
    console.log("Connection open...");
};
```

By the time the open event fires, the protocol handshake has completed and the WebSocket is ready to send and receive data. If your application receives an open event, you can be sure that a WebSocket server successfully handled the connection request and has agreed to communicate with your application.

WebSocket Event: Message

WebSocket messages contain the data from the server. You may also have heard of WebSocket frames, which comprise WebSocket messages. We'll discuss the concept of messages and frames in more depth in Chapter 3. For the purposes of understanding

17

how messages work with the API, the WebSocket API only exposes complete messages, not WebSocket frames. The message event fires when messages are received. The corresponding callback to the message event is called onmessage.

Listing 2-5 shows a message handler receiving a text message and displaying the content of the message.

Listing 2-5. Sample Message Event Handler for Text Messages

```
// Event handler for receiving text messages
ws.onmessage = function(e) {
   if(typeof e.data === "string"){
      console.log("String message received", e, e.data);
   } else {
      console.log("Other message received", e, e.data);
   }
};
```

In addition to text, WebSocket messages can handle binary data, which are handled as Blob messages, as shown in Listing 2-6 or as ArrayBuffer messages, as shown in Listing 2-7. Because the application setting for the WebSocket message binary data type affects incoming binary messages, you must decide the type you want to use for incoming binary data on the client before reading the data.

Listing 2-6. Sample Message Event Handler for Blob Messages

```
// Set binaryType to blob (Blob is the default.)
ws.binaryType = "blob";

// Event handler for receiving Blob messages
ws.onmessage = function(e) {
   if(e.data instanceof Blob){
      console.log("Blob message received", e.data);
      var blob = new Blob(e.data);
   }
};
```

Listing 2-7 shows a message handler checking and handling for ArrayBuffer messages.

Listing 2-7. Sample Message Event Handler for ArrayBuffer Messages

```
// Set binaryType to ArrayBuffer messages
ws.binaryType = "arraybuffer";

// Event handler for receiving ArrayBuffer messages
ws.onmessage = function(e) {
   if(e.data instanceof ArrayBuffer){
      console.log("ArrayBuffer Message Received", + e.data);
      // e.data is an ArrayBuffer. Create a byte view of that object.
      var a = new Uint8Array(e.data);
   }
};
```

18

WebSocket Event: Error

The error event fires in response to unexpected failures. The corresponding callback to the error event is called onerror. Errors also cause WebSocket connections to close. If you receive an error event, you can expect a close event to follow shortly. The code and reason in the close event can sometimes tell you what caused the error. The error event handler is a good place to call your reconnection logic to the server and handle the exceptions coming from the WebSocket object. Listing 2-8 shows an example of how to listen for error events.

Listing 2-8. Sample Error Event Handler

```
// Event handler for errors in the WebSocket object
ws.onerror = function(e) {
   console.log("WebSocket Error: " , e);
   //Custom function for handling errors
   handleErrors(e);
};
```

WebSocket Event: Close

The close event fires when the WebSocket connection is closed. The corresponding callback to the close event is called onclose. Once the connection is closed, the client and server can no longer receive or send messages.

■ **Note**   The WebSocket specification also defines ping and pong frames that can be used for keep-alive, heartbeats, network status probing, latency instrumentation, and so forth, but the WebSocket API does not currently expose these features. Although the browser receives a ping frame, it will not fire a visible ping event on the corresponding WebSocket. Instead, the browser will respond automatically with a pong frame. However, a browser-initiated ping that is unanswered by a pong after some period of time may also trigger the connection close event. Chapter 8 covers WebSocket pings and pongs in more detail.

You also trigger the onclose event handler when you call the close() method and terminate the connection with the server, as shown in Listing 2-9.

Listing 2-9. Sample Close Event Handler

```
// Event handler for closed connections
ws.onclose = function(e) {
   console.log("Connection closed", e);
};
```

The WebSocket close event is triggered when the connection is closed, which can be due to a number of reasons such as a connection failure or a successful WebSocket closing handshake. The WebSocket object attribute readyState reflects the status of the connection (2 for closing or 3 for closed).

The close event has three useful properties you can use for error handling and recovery: wasClean, code, and error. The wasClean property is a boolean indicating whether the connection was closed cleanly. The property is true if the WebSocket closed in response to a close frame from the server. If the connection closes due to some other reason (for example, because underlying TCP connection closed), the wasClean property is false. The code and reason properties indicate the status of the closing handshake conveyed from the server. These properties are symmetrical with the code and reason arguments given in the WebSocket.close() method, which we'll describe in detail later in this chapter. In Chapter 3, we will cover the closing codes and their meanings as we discuss the WebSocket Protocol.

⬛ **Note**   For more details about WebSocket events, see the WebSocket API specification at http://www.w3.org/TR/websockets/.

WebSocket Methods

WebSocket objects have two methods: send() and close().

WebSocket Method: send()

Once you establish a full-duplex, bidirectional connection between your client and server using WebSocket, you can invoke the send() method while the connection is open (that is, after the onopen listener is called and before the onclose listener is called). You use the send() method to send messages from your client to the server. After sending one or more messages, you can leave the connection open or call the close() method to terminate the connection.

Listing 2-10 is an example of how you can send a text message to the server.

Listing 2-10. Sending a Text Message Over WebSocket

```
// Send a text message
ws.send("Hello WebSocket!");
```

The send() method transmits data when the connection is open. If the connection is not available or closed, it throws an exception about the invalid connection state. A common mistake people make when starting out with the WebSocket API is attempting to send messages before the connection is open, as shown in Listing 2-11.

Listing 2-11. Attempting to Send Messages Before Opening a Connection

```
// Open a connection and try to send a message. (This will not work!)
var ws = new WebSocket("ws://echo.websocket.org")
ws.send("Initial data");
```

Listing 2-11 will not work because the connection is not yet open. Instead, you should wait for the open event before sending your first message on a newly constructed WebSocket, as shown in Listing 2-12.

Listing 2-12. Waiting for the Open Event Before Sending a Message

```
// Wait until the open event before calling send().
var ws = new WebSocket("ws://echo.websocket.org")
ws.onopen = function(e) {
   ws.send("Initial data");
}
```

If you want to send messages in response another event, you can check the WebSocket readyState property and choose to send the data only while the socket is open, as shown in Listing 2-13.

Listing 2-13. Checking the readyState Property for an Open WebSocket

```
// Handle outgoing data. Send on a WebSocket if that socket is open.
function myEventHandler(data) {
   if (ws.readyState === WebSocket.OPEN) {
      // The socket is open, so it is ok to send the data.
      ws.send(data);
   } else {
      // Do something else in this case.
      //Possibly ignore the data or enqueue it.
   }
}
```

In addition to the text (string) messages, the WebSocket API allows you to send binary data, which is especially useful to implement binary protocols. Such binary protocols can be standard Internet protocols typically layered on top of TCP, where the payload can be either a Blob or an ArrayBuffer. Listing 2-14 is an example of how you can send a binary message over WebSocket.

▓ **Note**   Chapter 6 shows an example of how you can send binary data over WebSocket.

Listing 2-14. Sending a Binary Message Over WebSocket

```
// Send a Blob
var blob = new Blob("blob contents");
ws.send(blob);

// Send an ArrayBuffer
var a = new Uint8Array([8,6,7,5,3,0,9]);
ws.send(a.buffer);
```

Blob objects are particularly useful when combined with the JavaScript File API for sending and receiving files, mostly multimedia files, images, video, and audio. The sample code at the end of this chapter uses the WebSocket API in conjunction with the File API, reads the content of a file, and sends it as a WebSocket message.

WebSocket Method: `close()`

To close the WebSocket connection or to terminate an attempt to connect, use the `close()` method. If the connection is already closed, then the method does nothing. After calling `close()`, you cannot send any more data on the closed WebSocket. Listing 2-15 shows an example of the `close()` method:

Listing 2-15. Calling the `close()` Method

```
// Close the WebSocket connection
ws.close();
```

You can optionally pass two arguments to the `close()` method: code (a numerical status code) and reason (a text string). Passing these arguments transmits information to the server about why the client closed the connection. We will discuss the status codes and reasons in greater detail in Chapter 3, when we cover the WebSocket closing handshake. Listing 2-16 shows an example of calling the `close()` method with an argument.

Listing 2-16. Calling the `close()` Method with a Reason

```
// Close the WebSocket connection because the session has ended successfully
ws.close(1000, "Closing normally");
```

Listing 2-16 uses code 1000, which means, as it states in the code, that the connection is closing normally.

WebSocket Object Attributes

There are several WebSocket Object attributes you can use to provide more information about the WebSocket object: readyState, bufferedAmount, and protocol.

WebSocket Object Attribute: readyState

The WebSocket object reports the state of the connection through the read-only attribute readyState, which you've already learned a bit about in the previous sections. This attribute automatically changes according to the connection state, and provides useful information about the WebSocket connection.

Table 2-1 describes the four different values to which the readyState attribute can be set to describe connection state.

Table 2-1. *readyState Attributes, Values, and Status Descriptions*

Attribute Constant	Value	Status
WebSocket.CONNECTING	0	The connection is in progress but has not been established.
WebSocket.OPEN	1	The connection has been established. Messages can flow between the client and server.
WebSocket.CLOSING	2	The connection is going through the closing handshake.
WebSocket.CLOSED	3	The connection has been closed or could not be opened.

(World Wide Web Consortium, 2012)

As the WebSocket API describes, when the WebSocket object is first created, its readyState is 0, indicating that the socket is connecting. Understanding the current state of the WebSocket connection can help you debug your application, such as to ensure you've opened the WebSocket connection before you've attempted to start sending requests to the server. This information can also be useful in understanding the lifespan of your connection.

WebSocket Object Attribute: bufferedAmount

When designing your application, you may want to check for the amount of data buffered for transmission to the server, particularly if the client application transports large amounts of data to the server. Even though calling send() is instant, actually transmitting that data over the Internet is not. Browsers will buffer outgoing data on behalf of your client application, so you can call send() as often as you like with as much data as you like. If you want to know how quickly that data is draining out to the network, however, the WebSocket object can tell you the size of the buffer. You can use the bufferedAmount attribute to check the number of bytes that have been queued but not yet transmitted to the server. The values reported in this attribute do not include framing overhead incurred by the protocol or buffering done by the operating system or network hardware.

Listing 2-17 shows an example of how to use the bufferedAmount attribute to send updates every second; if the network cannot handle that rate, it adjusts accordingly.

Listing 2-17. bufferedAmount Example

```
// 10k max buffer size.
var THRESHOLD = 10240;

// Create a New WebSocket connection
var ws = new WebSocket("ws://echo.websocket.org/updates");

// Listen for the opening event
ws.onopen = function () {
```

```
   // Attempt to send update every second.
   setInterval( function() {
      // Send only if the buffer is not full
      if (ws.bufferedAmount < THRESHOLD) {
         ws.send(getApplicationState());
      }
   }, 1000);
};
```

Using the bufferedAmount attribute can be useful for throttling the rate at which applications send data to the server avoiding network saturation.

░ **Pro Tip**   You may want to examine the WebSocket object's bufferedAmount attribute before attempting to close the connection to determine if any data has yet to be transmitted from the application.

WebSocket Object Attribute: protocol

In our previous discussion about the WebSocket constructor, we mentioned the protocol argument that lets the server know which protocol the client understands and can use over WebSocket. The WebSocket object protocol attribute provides another piece of useful information about the WebSocket instance. The result of protocol negotiation between the client and the server is visible on the WebSocket object. The protocol attribute contains the name of the protocol chosen by the WebSocket server during the opening handshake. In other words, the protocol attribute tells you which protocol to use with a particular WebSocket. The protocol attribute is the empty string before the opening handshake completes and remains an empty string if the server does not choose one of the protocols offered by the client.

Putting It All Together

Now that we've walked through the WebSocket constructor, events, attributes, and methods, let's put together what we have learned about the WebSocket API. Here, we create a client application to communicate with a remote server over the Web and exchange data using WebSocket. Our sample JavaScript client uses the "Echo" server hosted at ws://echo.websocket.org, which receives and returns any message you send to the server. Using an Echo server can be useful for pure client-side testing, particularly for understanding how the WebSocket API interacts with the server.

First, we create the connection, then display on a web page the events triggered by our code, which come from the server. The page will display information about the client connecting to the server, sending and receiving messages to and from the server, then disconnecting from the server.

Listing 2-18 shows a complete example of communication and messaging with the server.

Listing 2-18. Complete Client Application Using the WebSocket API

```
<!DOCTYPE html>
<title>WebSocket Echo Client</title>
<h2>Websocket Echo Client</h2>

<div id="output"></div>
<script>

// Initialize WebSocket connection and event handlers

function setup() {
    output = document.getElementById("output");
    ws = new WebSocket("ws://echo.websocket.org/echo");

// Listen for the connection open event then call the sendMessage function
    ws.onopen = function(e) {
        log("Connected");
        sendMessage("Hello WebSocket!")
    }

// Listen for the close connection event
    ws.onclose = function(e) {
        log("Disconnected: " + e.reason);
    }

// Listen for connection errors
    ws.onerror = function(e) {
        log("Error ");
    }

// Listen for new messages arriving at the client
    ws.onmessage = function(e) {
        log("Message received: " + e.data);
        // Close the socket once one message has arrived.
        ws.close();
    }
}

// Send a message on the WebSocket.
function sendMessage(msg){
    ws.send(msg);
        log("Message sent");
    }

// Display logging information in the document.
function log(s) {
    var p = document.createElement("p");
    p.style.wordWrap = "break-word";
```

```
    p.textContent = s;
    output.appendChild(p);

    // Also log information on the javascript console
    console.log(s);
}

// Start running the example.
setup();
</script>
```

After running the web page, the output should look similar to the following:

```
WebSocket Sample Client


Connected


Message sent


Message received: Hello WebSocket!


Disconnected
```

If you see this output, congratulations! You've successfully created and executed your first sample WebSocket client application. If the example does not work, you'll need to investigate why it has failed. You may find useful information in the JavaScript console of your browser. It is possible, though increasingly unlikely, that your browser does not support WebSocket. While the latest versions of every major browser contain support for the WebSocket API and protocol, there are still some older browsers in use that do not have this support. The next section shows you how to ensure your browser supports WebSocket.

Checking for WebSocket Support

Since (surprisingly) not all web browsers support WebSocket natively yet, it's good practice to include in your code a way to determine the browser support and, if possible, provide a fallback. Most modern browsers support WebSocket, but depending on your users, you'll likely want to use one of these techniques to cover your bases.

░ **Note**   Chapter 8 discusses various WebSocket fallback and emulation options.

There are several ways to determine whether your own browser supports WebSocket. One handy tool to use to investigate your code is the web browser's JavaScript console. Each browser has a different way to initiate the JavaScript console. In Google Chrome, for example, you can open the console by choosing **View ➤ Developer ➤ Developer Tools**, then clicking **Console**. For more information about Chrome Developer Tools, see https://developers.google.com/chrome-developer-tools/docs/overview.

■ **Pro Tip**   Google's Chrome Developer Tools also enables you to inspect WebSocket traffic. To do so, in the Developer Tools panel, click Network, then at the bottom of the panel, click WebSockets. Appendix A covers useful WebSocket debugging tools in detail.

Open your browser's interactive JavaScript console and evaluate the expression window.WebSocket. If you see the WebSocket constructor object, this means your web browser supports WebSocket natively. If your browser supports WebSocket but your sample code does not work, you'll need to further debug your code. If you evaluate the same expression and it comes back blank or undefined, your browser does not support WebSocket natively.

To ensure your WebSocket application works in browsers that do not support WebSocket, you'll need to look at fallback or emulation strategies. You can write this yourself (which is very complex), use a polyfill (a JavaScript library that replicates the standard API for older browsers), or use a WebSocket vendor like Kaazing, which supports WebSocket emulation that enables any browser (back to Microsoft Internet Explorer 6) to support the HTML5 WebSocket standard APIs. We'll discuss these options further in Chapter 8 as part of deploying your WebSocket application to the enterprise.

As part of your application, you can add a conditional check for WebSocket support, as shown in Listing 2-19.

Listing 2-19. Client Code to Determine WebSocket Support in a Browser

```
if (window.WebSocket){
    console.log("This browser supports WebSocket!");
} else {
    console.log("This browser does not support WebSocket.");
}
```

■ **Note**   There are many online resources that describe HTML5 and WebSocket compatibility with browsers, including mobile browsers. Two such resources are http://caniuse.com/ and http://html5please.com/.

Using HTML5 Media with WebSocket

As part of HTML5 and the Web platform, the WebSocket API was designed to work well with all HTML5 features. The data types that you can send and receive with the API are broadly useful for transferring application data and media. Strings, of course, allow you to represent web data formats like XML and JSON. The binary types integrate with APIs like drag-and-drop, FileReader, WebGL, and the Web Audio API.

Let's take a look at using HTML5 media with WebSocket. Listing 2-20 shows a complete client application using HTML5 Media with WebSocket. You can create your own HTML file based on this code.

▓ **Note** To build (or simply follow) the examples in this book, you can choose to use the virtual machine (VM) we've created that contains all the code, libraries, and servers we use in our examples. Refer to Appendix B for instructions on how to download, install, and start the VM.

Listing 2-20. Complete Client Application Using HTML5 Media with WebSocket

```
<!DOCTYPE html>
<title>WebSocket Image Drop</title>
<h1>Drop Image Here</h1>
<script>

// Initialize WebSocket connection
var wsUrl = "ws://echo.websocket.org/echo";
var ws = new WebSocket(wsUrl);
ws.onopen = function() {
 console.log("open");
}

// Handle binary image data received on the WebSocket
ws.onmessage = function(e) {
   var blob = e.data;
   console.log("message: " + blob.size + " bytes");
   // Work with prefixed URL API
  if (window.webkitURL) {
     URL = webkitURL;
   }

   var uri = URL.createObjectURL(blob);
   var img = document.createElement("img");
   img.src = uri;
   document.body.appendChild(img);
}
```

```
// Handle drop event
document.ondrop = function(e) {
   document.body.style.backgroundColor = "#fff";
   try {
      e.preventDefault();
      handleFileDrop(e.dataTransfer.files[0]);
      return false;
   } catch(err) {
      console.log(err);
   }
}

// Provide visual feedback for the drop area
document.ondragover = function(e) {
   e.preventDefault();
   document.body.style.backgroundColor = "#6fff41";
}
document.ondragleave = function() {
  document.body.style.backgroundColor = "#fff";
}

// Read binary file contents and send them over WebSocket
function handleFileDrop(file) {
   var reader = new FileReader();
   reader.readAsArrayBuffer(file);
   reader.onload = function() {
      console.log("sending: " + file.name);
      ws.send(reader.result);
   }
}
</script>
```

Open this file in your favorite modern browser. Take a look at your browser's JavaScript console while the WebSocket connection opens. Figure 2-1 shows the client application running in Mozilla Firefox. Notice that, at the bottom of this figure, we've displayed the JavaScript console, available in Firebug (a powerful web development and debugging tool available at http://getfirebug.com).

Drop Image Here

Figure 2-1. *Client application using HTML5 Media with WebSocket displaying in Mozilla Firefox*

Now, try dragging and dropping an image file onto this page. After you finish dropping the image file onto the page, you should see the image rendered on the web page, as shown in Figure 2-2. Notice how Firebug displays information about the image file being added to your page.

Figure 2-2. *Image (PNG) displayed in the client application using HTML5 Media with WebSocket in Mozilla Firefox*

> ■ **Note** The server `websocket.org` currently only accepts small messages, so this example will only work with image files less than 65kb in size, though this limit may change. You can experiment with larger media on your own servers.

The "wow" factor of this demo may be diminished by the fact that the media is originating from the same browser where it is ultimately displayed. You could accomplish the same visual result with AJAX or even without the network at all. Things get really interesting when a client or server sends some media data out that is displayed by a different browser—even *thousands* of other browsers! The same mechanics of reading and displaying binary image data work in a broadcast scenario just the same as in this simplified echo demo.

Summary

In this chapter, you learned about the various aspects of the WebSocket API, which enables you to initiate a WebSocket connection from a client application running in a browser and send messages from a server over a WebSocket connection to your client. You learned the basic concepts behind the WebSocket API, including events, messages, and attributes, as well as saw a few examples of the API in action. You also learned how to create your own WebSocket application with a publicly available WebSocket Echo server, which you can use for further testing of your own applications. For an authoritative definition of the interface, see the full WebSocket API specification at `http://www.w3.org/TR/websockets/`.

In Chapter 3, you will learn about the WebSocket Protocol and step through constructing your own basic WebSocket server.

CHAPTER 3

▨ ▨ ▨

The WebSocket Protocol

WebSocket is a network protocol that defines how servers and clients communicate over the Web. Protocols are agreed-upon rules for communication. The suite of protocols that comprise the Internet is published by the IETF, the Internet Engineering Task Force. The IETF publishes Requests for Comments, called RFCs, which precisely specify protocols, including RFC 6455: The WebSocket Protocol. RFC 6455 was published in December 2011 and contains the exact rules that must be followed when implementing a WebSocket client or server.

In the previous chapter, we explored the WebSocket API, which allows applications to interact with the WebSocket Protocol. In this chapter, we take you through a brief history of the Internet and protocols, why the WebSocket Protocol was created, and how it works. We use network tools to observe and learn about WebSocket network traffic. Using an example WebSocket server written in JavaScript with Node.js, we examine how WebSocket handshakes establish WebSocket connections, how messages are encoded and decoded, and how connections are kept alive and closed. Finally, we use this example WebSocket server to remote control several browsers at the same time.

Before the WebSocket Protocol

To better understand the WebSocket Protocol, let's look at some of the historical context by taking a quick tour to see how WebSocket fits into an important family of protocols.

PROTOCOLS!

Protocols are one of the greatest parts of computing. They span programming languages, operating systems, and hardware architectures. They allow components written by different people and operated by different agents to communicate amongst themselves from across the room or across the world. So many of the success stories in open, interoperable systems are due to well-designed protocols.

Before the introduction of the World Wide Web and its constituent technologies like HTML and HTTP, the Internet was a very different network. For one, it was *much* smaller and, for another, it was essentially a network of peers. Two protocols were and still are prevalent when communicating between Internet hosts: the Internet Protocol (IP, which is responsible for simply transmitting packets between two hosts on the Internet) and the Transmission Control Protocol (TCP, which can be viewed as a pipe stretched across the Internet and carries a reliable stream of bytes in each direction between two endpoints). Together, TCP over IP (TCP/IP) has historically been and continues to be the core transport layer protocol used by innumerable network applications.

A Brief History of the Internet

In the beginning, there was TCP/IP communication between Internet hosts. In this scenario, either host can establish new connections. Once a TCP connection is established, either host can send data at any time, as shown in Figure 3-1.

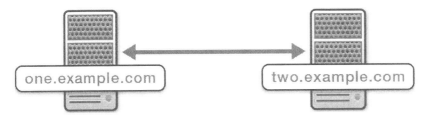

Figure 3-1. *TCP/IP communication between Internet hosts*

Any other feature you might want in a network protocol must be built on top of the transport protocol. These higher layers are called *application protocols*. For example, two important application layer protocols that predate the Web are IRC for chat and Telnet for remote terminal access. IRC and Telnet clearly require asynchronous bidirectional communication. Clients must receive prompt notification when another user sends a chat message or when a remote application prints a line of output. Since these protocols typically run over TCP, asynchronous bidirectional communication is always available. IRC and Telnet sessions maintain persistent connections on which the client and server can send freely to each other at any time. TCP/IP also serves as the foundation for two other important protocols: HTTP and WebSocket. Before we get ahead of ourselves, though, let's take brief look at HTTP.

The Web and HTTP

In 1991, the World Wide Web project was announced in its earliest public form. The Web is a system of linked hypertext documents using Universal Resource Locators (URLs). At the time, URLs were a major innovation. The U in URL, standing for universal, points to the then-revolutionary idea that all hypertext documents could be interconnected. HTML documents on the Web link to other documents by URLs. It makes sense, then, that the protocol of the Web is tailored to fetching resources. HTTP is a simple synchronous request-response style protocol for document transfer.

The earliest web applications used forms and full page reloads. Every time a user submitted information, the browser would submit a form and fetch a new page. Every time there was updated information to display, the user or browser had to refresh an entire page to fetch a complete resource by using HTTP.

With JavaScript and the XMLHttpRequest API, a set of techniques called AJAX were developed to allow more seamless applications that did not have abrupt transitions during every interaction. AJAX let applications fetch just the resource data of interest and update a page in place without navigation. With AJAX, the network protocol is still HTTP; the data is only sometimes, but not always, XML despite the XMLHttpRequest name.

The Web has become pretty popular. So popular, in fact, that many confuse the Web with the Internet since the Web is often the only significant Internet application they use. NAT (Network Address Translation), HTTP proxies, and firewalls have also become increasingly common. Today, many Internet users do not have publicly visible IP addresses. There are many reasons why users do not each have unique IP addresses, including security measures, overcrowding, and simple lack of necessity. The lack of addresses prevents addressability; for example, worms that require public addresses cannot access unaddressed users. Additionally, there are not enough IPv4 addresses for all Web users. NAT allows users to share public IP addresses and still surf the Web. Finally, the dominant protocol, HTTP, does not require addressable clients. HTTP works fairly well for interactions driven by client applications, since the client initiates every HTTP request, as shown in Figure 3-2:

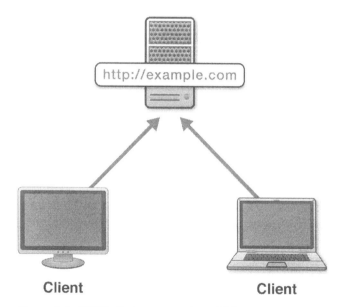

Figure 3-2. *HTTP clients connected to a Web server*

Essentially, HTTP made the Web possible with its built-in support for text (thus supporting our interconnected HTML pages), URLs, and HTTPS (secure HTTP over Transport Layer Security (TLS)). However, in some ways, HTTP also caused the Internet to *regress* due to its popularity. Because HTTP does not require addressable clients, addressing in the Web world is asymmetrical. Browsers can address resources on servers via URLs, but there is no way for a server-side application to proactively send a resource to a client. Clients can only make requests, and the server can only respond to outstanding requests. In this asymmetrical world, protocols that require full-duplex communication just don't work as well.

One way to work around that limitation is to have the client open HTTP requests just in case the server has an update to share. The umbrella term for using HTTP requests to reverse the flow of notifications is called "Comet." As we discussed in the earlier chapters, Comet is basically a set of techniques that stretch HTTP to the limit with polling, long polling, and streaming. These techniques essentially simulate some of TCP's capabilities in order to address the same server-to-client use cases. Because of the mismatch between synchronous HTTP and these asynchronous applications, Comet tends to be complicated, non-standard, and inefficient.

░ **Note**   In server-to-server communication, each host can address the other. It is possible for one server to simply make an HTTP request to the other when there is new data available, which is the case with the PubSubHubbub protocol for server-to-server feed update notification. PubSubHubbub is an open protocol that extends RSS and Atom, and enables publish/subscribe communication between HTTP servers. While server-to-server communication is possible with WebSocket, this book focuses on client–server communication in real-time web applications.

Introducing the WebSocket Protocol

This short history of the Internet lesson brings us to today. Now, web applications are quite powerful with significant client-side state and logic. Often, modern web applications require bidirectional communication. Immediate notification of updates is more the rule than the exception, and users increasingly expect responsive real-time interactivity. Let's take a look at what WebSocket gives us.

WebSocket: Internet Capabilities for Web Applications

WebSocket preserves many of the things we like about HTTP for web applications (URLs, HTTP security, easier message based data model, and built-in support for text) while enabling other network architectures and communication patterns. Like TCP, WebSocket is asynchronous and can be used as a transport layer for higher-level protocols. WebSocket is a good base for messaging protocols, chat, server notifications, pipelined and multiplexed protocols, custom protocols, compact binary protocols, and other standard protocols for interoperating with Internet servers.

WebSocket provides TCP-style network capabilities to web applications. Addressing is still unidirectional. Servers can send clients data asynchronously, but only when there is an open WebSocket connection. WebSocket connections are always established from the client to the server. A WebSocket server can also act as a WebSocket client. However, with WebSocket, web clients like browsers cannot accept connections that they did not initiate. Figure 3-3 shows WebSocket clients connected to a server, where either the client or the server can send data at any time.

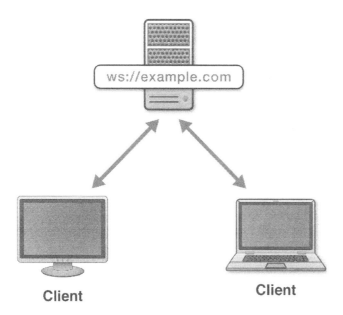

Figure 3-3. *WebSocket clients connected to a server*

WebSocket bridges the world of the Web and the world of the Internet (or more specifically, TCP/IP). Asynchronous protocols that were not previously easy to use with web applications can now easily communicate using WebSocket. Table 3-1 compares the main areas of TCP, HTTP, and WebSocket.

Table 3-1. *Comparison of TCP, HTTP, and WebSocket*

Feature	TCP	HTTP	WebSocket
Addressing	IP address and port	URL	URL
Simultaneous transmission	Full duplex	Half duplex	Full duplex
Content	Byte streams	MIME messages	Text and binary messages
Message boundaries	No	Yes	Yes
Connection oriented	Yes	No	Yes

TCP only communicates byte streams, so message boundaries must be represented in a higher-level protocol. One very common mistake made by beginning socket programmers using TCP is assuming that every call to send() will result in one successful receive. While this may happen to be true for simple tests, when load and latency vary, the bytes sent on a TCP socket will be unpredictably fragmented. TCP data can be spread over multiple IP packets or combined into fewer packets at the discretion of the operating system. The only guarantee in TCP is that the individual bytes that arrive on the receiving side will arrive in order. Unlike TCP, WebSocket transmits a sequence of discrete messages. With WebSocket, multi-byte messages will arrive in whole and in order, just like HTTP. Because message boundaries are built into the WebSocket Protocol, it is possible to send and receive separate messages and avoid common fragmentation mistakes.

It bears mentioning that before the Internet, another networking model was being followed: Open Systems Interconnection (OSI), which includes seven layers: physical, data link, network, transport, session, presentation, and application. However, while the terminology may be similar, OSI was not designed with the Internet in mind. The TCP/IP model, which was designed for the Internet, comprises just four layers: link, Internet, transport, and application, and is the model that drives the Internet today.

IP is at the Internet layer and TCP layers on top of IP at the transport layer. WebSocket layers on top of TCP (and therefore IP), and is also considered a transport layer because you can layer application-level protocols on top of WebSocket.

Inspecting WebSocket Traffic

In Chapter 2, we used the WebSocket API without really seeing what was happening at the network level. If you want to see WebSocket traffic flowing over a network, you can use tools like Wireshark (http://www.wireshark.org/) or tcpdump (http://www.tcpdump.org/) and inspect what's inside the communication stack. Wireshark enables you to "dissect" the WebSocket protocol, which lets you view the parts of the WebSocket Protocol we'll discuss later in this chapter (for example, opcodes, flags, and payloads) in a convenient UI, as shown in Figure 3-4. It will even display unmasked versions of messages sent from WebSocket clients. We'll discuss masking later in this chapter.

░ **Note** Appendix A covers WebSocket traffic debugging tools in detail.

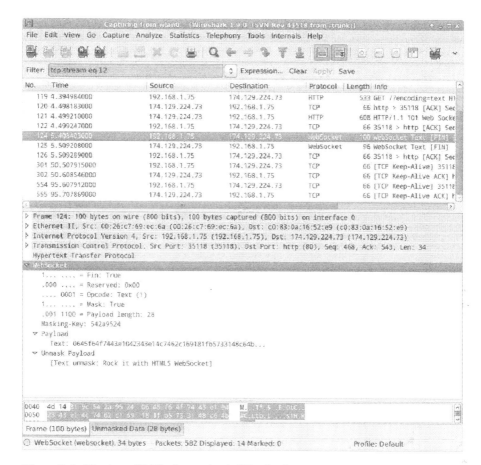

Figure 3-4. *Viewing a WebSocket session in Wireshark*

WebKit (the browser engine that powers Google Chrome and Apple Safari) also recently added support for inspecting WebSocket traffic. In the latest versions of the Chrome browser, you can see WebSocket messages in the Network tab of the Developer Tools. Figure 3-5 shows this must-have tool for developing with WebSocket.

Figure 3-5. *Using Google Chrome Developer Tools to view a WebSocket session*

We highly recommend using these tools to watch WebSockets in action, not only to learn about protocols, but also to better understand what is happening during the WebSocket session.

The WebSocket Protocol

Let's take a closer look at the WebSocket Protocol. For each part of the protocol, we will look at JavaScript code to handle that particular syntax. Afterward, we will combine these snippets into an example server library and two simple applications.

The WebSocket Opening Handshake

Every WebSocket connection begins with an HTTP request. This request is much like any other, except that it includes a special header: Upgrade. The Upgrade header indicates that the client would like to upgrade the connection to a different protocol. In this case, the different protocol is WebSocket.

Let's look at an example handshake recorded during a connection to ws://echo.websocket.org/echo. Until the handshake completes, a WebSocket session conforms to the HTTP/1.1 protocol. The client sends the HTTP request shown in Listing 3-1.

Listing 3-1. HTTP Request from the Client

```
GET /echo HTTP/1.1
Host: echo.websocket.org
Origin: http://www.websocket.org
Sec-WebSocket-Key: 7+C600xYyb0v2zmJ69RQsw==
Sec-WebSocket-Version: 13
Upgrade: websocket
```

Listing 3-2 shows the server sending back the response.

Listing 3-2. HTTP Response from the Server

```
101 Switching Protocols
Connection: Upgrade
Date: Wed, 20 Jun 2012 03:39:49 GMT
Sec-WebSocket-Accept: fYoqiH14DgI+5ylEMwM2sOLzOiO=
Server: Kaazing Gateway
Upgrade: WebSocket
```

Figure 3-6 illustrates the HTTP request upgrade to WebSocket from the client to the server, also known as the WebSocket opening handshake.

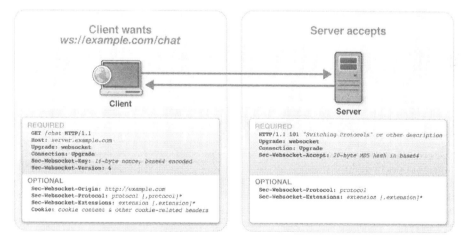

Figure 3-6. *Example of a WebSocket opening handshake*

Figure 3-6 shows the required and optional headers. Some headers are strictly required and must be present and precise for a WebSocket connection to succeed. Other headers in this handshake are optional but allowed because the handshake is an HTTP request and response. After a successful upgrade, the syntax of the connection switches over to the data-framing format used to represent WebSocket messages. Connections will not succeed unless the server responds with the 101 response code, Upgrade header, and Sec-WebSocket-Accept header. The value of the Sec-WebSocket-Accept response header is derived from the Sec-WebSocket-Key request header and contains a special key response that must match exactly what the client expects.

Computing the Key Response

To successfully complete the handshake, the WebSocket server must respond with a computed key. This response shows that the server understands the WebSocket Protocol specifically. Without the exact response, it might be possible to dupe some unsuspecting HTTP server into upgrading a connection accidentally!

This response function takes the key value from the Sec-WebSocket-Key header sent by the client and returns the computed value that the client expects in the returning Sec-WebSocket-Accept header. Listing 3-3 uses the Node.js crypto API to compute the SHA1 hash of the combined key and suffix:

Listing 3-3. Computing the Key Response Using the Node.jspto API Crypto API

```
var KEY_SUFFIX = "258EAFA5-E914-47DA-95CA-C5AB0DC85B11";
var hashWebSocketKey = function(key) {
   var sha1 = crypto.createHash("sha1");
   sha1.update(key + KEY_SUFFIX, "ascii");
   return sha1.digest("base64");
   }
```

▨ **Note**   The KEY_SUFFIX in Listing 3-3 is a constant key suffix included in the protocol specification that every WebSocket server must know.

In the WebSocket opening handshake and computing the key response, the WebSocket protocol relies on Sec- headers that are defined in RFC 6455. Table 3-2 describes these WebSocket Sec- Headers.

Table 3-2. *WebSocket Sec- Headers and Their Descriptions (RFC 6455)*

Header	Description
Sec-WebSocket-Key	Can only appear once in an HTTP request.
	Used in the opening WebSocket handshake from the client to the server to prevent cross-protocol attacks. See Sec-WebSocket-Accept.
Sec-WebSocket-Accept	Can only appear once in an HTTP response.
	Used in the opening WebSocket handshake from the server to the client, to confirm that the server understands the WebSocket protocol.
Sec-WebSocket-Extensions	May appear multiple times in an HTTP request (which is logically the same as a single Sec-WebSocket-Extensions header field that contains all values), but can only appear once in an HTTP response.
	Used in the WebSocket opening handshake from the client to the server, and then from the server to the client. This header helps the client and server agree on a set of protocol-level extensions to use for the duration of the connection.
Sec-WebSocket-Protocol	Used in the opening WebSocket handshake from the client to the server, then from the server to negotiate a subprotocol. This header advertises the protocols that a client-side application can use. The server uses the same header to select at most one of those protocols.
Sec-Websocket-Version	Used in the opening WebSocket handshake from the client to the server to indicate version compatibility. The version for RFC 6455 is always 13. The server responds with this header if it does not support the version of the protocol requested by the client. In that case, the header sent by the server lists the versions it does support. This only happens if the client predates RFC 6455.

Message Format

While a WebSocket connection is open, the client and server can send messages to each other at any time. These messages are represented on the network with a binary syntax that marks the boundaries between messages and includes concise type information. More precisely, these binary headers mark the boundaries between something else, called *frames*. Frames are partial data that can be combined to form messages. You may see "frame" and "message" used interchangeably in discussions about WebSocket. These terms are both used because it is (at least currently) rare to use more than one frame per message. Also, in early drafts of the protocol frames *were* messages, and the message representation on the wire was called framing.

You'll recall from Chapter 2, that the WebSocket API does not expose frame-level information to applications. It is possible to deal with sub-message data units at the protocol level, even though the API works in terms of messages. There is typically only one frame in a message, but a message can be composed of any number of frames. Servers could use different numbers of frames to begin delivering data before the entirety of the data is available.

Let's take a closer look at the aspects of the WebSocket frame. Figure 3-7 illustrates the WebSocket frame header.

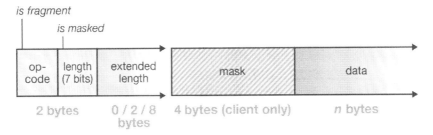

Figure 3-7. *WebSocket frame header*

WebSocket framing code is responsible for:

- Opcodes
- Length
- Decoding Text
- Masking
- Multi-frame messages

Opcodes

Every WebSocket message has an opcode specifying the type of the message payload. The opcode consists of the last four bits in the first byte of the frame header. Opcodes have a numerical value, as described in Table 3-3.

Table 3-3. *Defined Opcodes*

Opcode	Type of Message Payload	Description
1	Text	The data type of the message is text.
2	Binary	The data type of the message is binary.
8	Close	The client or server is sending a closing handshake to the server or client.
9	Ping	The client or server sends a ping to the server or client (see Chapter 8 for more details on using pings and pongs).
10 (hex 0xA)	Pong	The client or server sends a pong to the server or client (see Chapter 8 for more details on using pings and pongs).

With four bits used for opcodes, there can be up to 16 different values. The WebSocket Protocol defines only five opcodes, and the remaining opcodes are reserved for future use in extensions.

Length

The WebSocket Protocol encodes frame lengths using a variable number of bits, which allows small messages to use a compact encoding while still allowing the protocol to carry medium-sized and even very large messages. For messages under 126 bytes, the length is packed into one of the first two header bytes. For lengths between 126 and 216, two extra bytes are used. For messages larger than 126 bytes, eight bytes of length are included. The length is encoded in the last seven bits of the second byte of the frame header. The values 126 and 127 in that field are treated as special signals that additional bytes will follow to complete the encoded length.

Decoding Text

Text WebSocket messages are encoded with UCS Transformation Format—8 bit, or UTF-8. UTF-8 is a variable-length encoding for Unicode that is also backward compatible with seven-bit ASCII. UTF-8 is also the *only* encoding allowed in WebSocket text messages. Keeping the encoding to UTF-8 prevents the babel of different encodings found in the myriad "plain text" formats and protocols from hindering interoperability.

In Listing 3-4, the `deliverText` function uses the `buffer.toString()` API from Node.js to convert the payload of an incoming message to a JavaScript string. UTF-8 is the default encoding for `buffer.toString()`, but is specified here for clarity.

Listing 3-4. UTF-8 Text Encoding

```
case opcodes.TEXT:
   payload = buffer.toString("utf8");
```

Masking

WebSocket frames sent upstream from browsers to servers are "masked" to obfuscate their contents. The purpose of masking is not to prevent eavesdropping, but is intended for an unusual security reason and to improve compatibility with existing HTTP proxies. See Chapter 7 for further explanation of the sort of cross-protocol attacks that masking is intended to prevent.

The first bit of the second byte of the frame header indicates whether the frame is masked; the WebSocket Protocol requires that clients mask every frame they send. If there is a mask, it will be four bytes following the extended length portion of the frame header.

Every payload received by a WebSocket server is first unmasked before processing. Listing 3-5 shows a simple function that unmasks the payload portion of a WebSocket frame given four mask bytes.

Listing 3-5. Unmasking the Payload

```
var unmask = function(mask_bytes, buffer) {
   var payload = new Buffer(buffer.length);
   for (var i=0; i<buffer.length; i++) {
      payload[i] = mask_bytes[i%4] ^ buffer[i];
      }
   return payload;
}
```

After unmasking, the server has the original message contents: binary messages can be delivered directly, and text messages will be UTF-8 decoded and exposed through the server API as strings.

Multi-Frame Messages

The fin bit in the frame format allows for multi-frame messages or streaming of partially available messages, which may be fragmented or incomplete. To transmit an incomplete message, you can send a frame that has the fin bit set to zero. The last frame has the fin bit set to 1, indicating that the message ends with that frame's payload.

The WebSocket Closing Handshake

We looked at the WebSocket opening handshake earlier in this chapter. In human interactions, we often shake hands when first meeting. Sometimes we shake hands when parting, as well. The same is the case in this protocol. WebSocket connections always begin with the opening handshake, as that is the only way to initialize the conversation. On the Internet and other unreliable networks, connections can close at any time, so it is not possible to say that connections always end with a closing handshake. Sometimes the underlying TCP socket just closes abruptly. The closing handshake gracefully closes connections, allowing applications to tell the difference between intentionally and accidentally terminated connections.

When a WebSocket closes, the endpoint that is terminating the connection can send a numerical code and a reason string to indicate why it is choosing to close the socket. The code and reason are encoded in the payload of a frame with the close opcode (8). The code is represented as an unsigned 16-bit integer. The reason is a short UTF-8 encoded string. RFC 6455 defines several specific closing codes. Codes 1000–1015 are specified for use in the WebSocket connection layer. These codes indicate that something has failed in the network or in the protocol. Table 3-4 lists the codes in this range, their descriptions, and scenarios in which each code might be applicable.

Table 3-4. *Defined WebSocket Closed Codes*

Code	Description	When to Use this Code
1000	Normal Close	Send this code when your session has successfully completed.
1001	Going Away	Send this code when closing the connection because the application is going away and there is no expectation that a follow-up connection will be attempted. The server may be shutting down or the client application may be closing.
1002	Protocol Error	Send this code when closing the connection due to a protocol error.
1003	Unacceptable Data Type	Send this code when your application receives a message of an unexpected type that it cannot handle.
1004	Reserved	Do not send this code. According to RFC 6455, this status code is reserved and may be defined in the future.
1005	Reserved	Do not send this code. The WebSocket API uses this code to indicate that no code was received.
1006	Reserved	Do not send this code. The Websocket API uses this code to indicate that the connection has closed abnormally.
1007	Invalid Data	Send this code after receiving a message for which the formatting does not match the message type. If a text message ever contains malformed UTF-8 data, the connection should close with this code.
1008	Message Violates Policy	Send this code when your application terminates the connection for a reason not covered by another code or when you do not wish to disclose the reason a message cannot be handled.

(continued)

47

Table 3-4. (*continued*)

Code	Description	When to Use this Code
1009	Message Too Large	Send this code when receiving a message that is too large for your application to handle. (Remember, frames can have payload lengths up to 64 bits long. Even if you have a big server, some messages are still too large.)
1010	Extension Required	Send this code from the client (browser) when your application requires one or more specific extensions that the server did not negotiate.
1011	Unexpected Condition	Send this code when your application cannot continue handling the connection for an unforeseen reason.
1015	TLS Failure (reserved)	Do not send this code. The WebSocket API uses this code to indicate when TLS has failed before the WebSocket handshake.

■ **Note** Chapter 2 describes how the WebSocket API uses the close codes. For additional information about the WebSocket API, see `http://www.w3.org/TR/websockets/`.

Other code ranges are reserved for specific purposes. Table 3-5 lists the four categories of close codes defined in RFC 6455.

Table 3-5. *WebSocket Close Code Ranges*

Code	Description	When to Use this Code
0-999	Prohibited	Codes below 1000 are invalid and can never be used for any purpose.
1000-2999	Reserved	These codes are reserved for use in extensions and revised versions of the WebSocket protocol itself. Use these codes as the standard prescribes. See Table 3-4.
3000-3999	Registration Required	These codes are intended for use by "libraries, frameworks, and applications." These codes should be publicly registered with IANA (Internet Assigned Numbers Authority).
4000-4999	Private	Use these codes for custom purposes in your applications. Because they are not registered, do not expect them to be widely understood by other WebSocket software.

Support for Other Protocols

The WebSocket Protocol supports higher-level protocols and protocol negotiation. Paradoxically, RFC 6455 refers to protocols you can use with WebSocket as "subprotocols," even though they are higher-level, fully formed protocols. As we mentioned in Chapter 2, throughout this book, we'll generally refer to protocols that you can use with WebSocket simply as "protocols" to avoid confusion.

In Chapter 2, we explained how to negotiate higher-layer protocols with the WebSocket API. At the network level, these protocols are negotiated using the Sec-WebSocket-Protocol header. Protocol names are header values sent from the client in the initial upgrade request:

```
Sec-WebSocket-Protocol: com.kaazing.echo, example.protocol.name
```

This header indicates that the client can use either protocol (com.kaazing.echo or example.protocol.name) and the server can choose which protocol to use. If you send this header in an upgrade request to ws://echo.websocket.org, the server response will include the following header:

```
Sec-WebSocket-Protocol: com.kaazing.echo
```

This response indicates that the server has elected to speak the com.kaazing.echo protocol. Selecting a protocol does not change the syntax of the WebSocket Protocol itself. Instead, these protocols are layered on top of the WebSocket Protocol to provide higher-level semantics for frameworks and applications. We will examine three different use cases of layering widely used, standards-based protocols on top of WebSocket in the subsequent chapters.

To simply extend the WebSocket Protocol, there is another mechanism, called extensions.

Extensions

Like protocols, extensions are negotiated with a `Sec-` header. The connecting client sends a `Sec-WebSocket-Extensions` header containing the names of the extension (or extensions) it supports.

▧ **Note**   While you cannot negotiate more than one protocol at a time, you can negotiate more than one extension at a time.

For example, Chrome might send the following header to indicate that it will accept an experimental compression extension:

```
Sec-WebSocket-Extensions: x-webkit-deflate-frame
```

Extensions are so named because they extend the WebSocket Protocol. Extensions can add new opcodes and data fields to the framing format. You may find it more difficult to deploy a new extension than a new protocol (or "subprotocol") because browser vendors must explicitly build in support for these extensions. You'll probably find it much easier to write a JavaScript library that implements a protocol than to wait for all browser vendors to standardize an extension and all users to update their browsers to the version supporting that extension.

Writing a WebSocket Server in JavaScript with Node.js

Now that we've examined the essentials of the WebSocket Protocol, let's step through writing our own WebSocket server. There are many existing implementations of the WebSocket Protocol; you may choose to use an existing implementation in your applications. However, you may need to write a new server or modify an existing server out of necessity or just because you can. Writing your own implementation of the WebSocket Protocol can be fun and illuminating, and can help you understand and evaluate other servers, clients, and libraries. Best of all, it can give you new insights on networking, communication, and the Web.

The example server in this chapter is written in JavaScript using the IO APIs provided by Node.js. We chose these technologies simply to limit the code samples in this book to a single language. Since you are likely using JavaScript with HTML5 for your front-end development, there is a good chance you will be able to read this code fluently, as well. Of course, it isn't necessary that you write your server in JavaScript, and there are strong reasons why you might choose another language. The fact that WebSocket is a language-agnostic protocol means you can select any programming language capable of listening on a socket and create a server.

We wrote this example to work with Node.js 0.8. It will not run with earlier versions of Node.js and may require some modification in the future if the Node APIs change. The websocket-example module combines the preceding code snippets and some additional code to form a WebSocket server. This example is not fully robust and production-ready, but it does serve as a simple, self-contained example of the protocol.

▨ **Note** To build (or simply follow) the examples in this book, you can choose to use the virtual machine (VM) we've created that contains all the code, libraries, and servers we use in our examples. Refer to Appendix B for instructions on how to download, install, and start the VM.

Building a Simple WebSocket Server

Listing 3-6 starts us off by building a simple WebSocket server. You can also open the file websocket-example.js to view the sample code.

Listing 3-6. WebSocket Server API Written in JavaScript with Node.js

```
// The Definitive Guide to HTML5 WebSocket
//   Example WebSocket server

// See The WebSocket Protocol for the official specification
// http://tools.ietf.org/html/rfc6455

var events = require("events");
var http = require("http");
var crypto = require("crypto");
var util = require("util");

// opcodes for WebSocket frames
// http://tools.ietf.org/html/rfc6455#section-5.2

var opcodes = { TEXT  : 1
    , BINARY: 2
    , CLOSE : 8
    , PING  : 9
    , PONG  : 10
};

var WebSocketConnection = function(req, socket, upgradeHead) {
    var self = this;

    var key = hashWebSocketKey(req.headers["sec-websocket-key"]);
```

```
    // handshake response
    // http://tools.ietf.org/html/rfc6455#section-4.2.2

    socket.write('HTTP/1.1 101 Web Socket Protocol Handshake\r\n' +
        'Upgrade: WebSocket\r\n' +
        'Connection: Upgrade\r\n' +
        'sec-websocket-accept: ' + key +
        '\r\n\r\n');

    socket.on("data", function(buf) {
        self.buffer = Buffer.concat([self.buffer, buf]);
        while(self._processBuffer()) {
        // process buffer while it contains complete frames
        }
    });

    socket.on("close", function(had_error) {
        if (!self.closed) {
            self.emit("close", 1006);
            self.closed = true;
        }
    });

    // initialize connection state

    this.socket = socket;
    this.buffer = new Buffer(0);
    this.closed = false;
}
util.inherits(WebSocketConnection, events.EventEmitter);

// Send a text or binary message on the WebSocket connection

WebSocketConnection.prototype.send = function(obj) {
    var opcode;
    var payload;
    if (Buffer.isBuffer(obj)) {
        opcode = opcodes.BINARY;
        payload = obj;
    } else if (typeof obj == "string") {
    opcode = opcodes.TEXT;
// create a new buffer containing the UTF-8 encoded string
    payload = new Buffer(obj, "utf8");
    } else {
        throw new Error("Cannot send object. Must be string or Buffer");
    }
    this._doSend(opcode, payload);
}
```

```
// Close the WebSocket connection

WebSocketConnection.prototype.close = function(code, reason) {
    var opcode = opcodes.CLOSE;
    var buffer;

// Encode close and reason

if (code) {
    buffer = new Buffer(Buffer.byteLength(reason) + 2);
    buffer.writeUInt16BE(code, 0);
    buffer.write(reason, 2);
    } else {
        buffer = new Buffer(0);
    }
    this._doSend(opcode, buffer);
    this.closed = true;
}

// Process incoming bytes

WebSocketConnection.prototype._processBuffer = function() {
    var buf = this.buffer;

    if (buf.length < 2) {
        // insufficient data read
        return;
    }

    var idx = 2;

    var b1 = buf.readUInt8(0);
    var fin = b1 & 0x80;
    var opcode = b1 & 0x0f;        // low four bits
    var b2 = buf.readUInt8(1);
    var mask = b2 & 0x80;
    var length = b2 & 0x7f;        // low 7 bits

    if (length > 125) {
        if (buf.length < 8) {
        // insufficient data read
        return;
    }

    if (length == 126) {
        length = buf.readUInt16BE(2);
        idx += 2;
        } else if (length == 127) {
```

```
      // discard high 4 bits because this server cannot handle huge lengths
      var highBits = buf.readUInt32BE(2);
      if (highBits != 0) {
      this.close(1009, "");
      }
      length = buf.readUInt32BE(6);
      idx += 8;
      }
   }

   if (buf.length < idx + 4 + length) {
      // insufficient data read
      return;
   }

   maskBytes = buf.slice(idx, idx+4);
   idx += 4;
   var payload = buf.slice(idx, idx+length);
   payload = unmask(maskBytes, payload);
   this._handleFrame(opcode, payload);

   this.buffer = buf.slice(idx+length);
   return true;
}

WebSocketConnection.prototype._handleFrame = function(opcode, buffer) {
var payload;
switch (opcode) {
   case opcodes.TEXT:
   payload = buffer.toString("utf8");
  this.emit("data", opcode, payload);
   break;
   case opcodes.BINARY:
   payload = buffer;
   this.emit("data", opcode, payload);
   break;
   case opcodes.PING:
   // Respond to pings with pongs
   this._doSend(opcodes.PONG, buffer);
   break;
   case opcodes.PONG:
   // Ignore pongs
    break;
    case opcodes.CLOSE:
   // Parse close and reason
   var code, reason;
   if (buffer.length >= 2) {
   code = buffer.readUInt16BE(0);
   reason = buffer.toString("utf8",2);
```

```
      }
      this.close(code, reason);
      this.emit("close", code, reason);
      break;
      default:
      this.close(1002, "unknown opcode");
      }
}

// Format and send a WebSocket message

WebSocketConnection.prototype._doSend = function(opcode, payload) {
    this.socket.write(encodeMessage(opcode, payload));
}

var KEY_SUFFIX = "258EAFA5-E914-47DA-95CA-C5AB0DC85B11";
var hashWebSocketKey = function(key) {
    var sha1 = crypto.createHash("sha1");
    sha1.update(key+KEY_SUFFIX, "ascii");
    return sha1.digest("base64");
}

var unmask = function(maskBytes, data) {
    var payload = new Buffer(data.length);
    for (var i=0; i<data.length; i++) {
       payload[i] = maskBytes[i%4] ^ data[i];
    }
    return payload;
}

var encodeMessage = function(opcode, payload) {
    var buf;
    // first byte: fin and opcode
    var b1 = 0x80 | opcode;
    // always send message as one frame (fin)

// Second byte: mask and length part 1
// Followed by 0, 2, or 8 additional bytes of continued length
var b2 = 0; // server does not mask frames
var length = payload.length;
if (length<126) {
    buf = new Buffer(payload.length + 2 + 0);
    // zero extra bytes
    b2 |= length;
    buf.writeUInt8(b1, 0);
    buf.writeUInt8(b2, 1);
    payload.copy(buf, 2);
} else if (length<(1<<16)) {
    buf = new Buffer(payload.length + 2 + 2);
```

```
   // two bytes extra
   b2 |= 126;
   buf.writeUInt8(b1, 0);
   buf.writeUInt8(b2, 1);
   // add two byte length
   buf.writeUInt16BE(length, 2);
   payload.copy(buf, 4);
} else {
   buf = new Buffer(payload.length + 2 + 8);
   // eight bytes extra
   b2 |= 127;
   buf.writeUInt8(b1, 0);
   buf.writeUInt8(b2, 1);
   // add eight byte length
   // note: this implementation cannot handle lengths greater than 2^32
   // the 32 bit length is prefixed with 0x0000
   buf.writeUInt32BE(0, 2);
   buf.writeUInt32BE(length, 6);
   payload.copy(buf, 10);
  }
return buf;
}

exports.listen = function(port, host, connectionHandler) {
   var srv = http.createServer(function(req, res) {
});

srv.on('upgrade', function(req, socket, upgradeHead) {
   var ws = new WebSocketConnection(req, socket, upgradeHead);
   connectionHandler(ws);
});

srv.listen(port, host);
};
```

Testing Our Simple WebSocket Server

Now, let's test our server. Echo is the "Hello, World" of networking, so the first thing we
will do with our new server API is create an server, as shown in Listing 3-7. Echo servers
simply respond with whatever the connected client sends. In this case, our WebSocket
echo server will respond with whatever WebSocket messages it receives.

Listing 3-7. Building an Echo Server Using Your New Server API

```
var websocket = require("./websocket-example");

websocket.listen(9999, "localhost", function(conn) {
   console.log("connection opened");
```

```
conn.on("data", function(opcode, data) {
    console.log("message: ", data);
    conn.send(data);
});

conn.on("close", function(code, reason) {
    console.log("connection closed: ", code, reason);
});
});
```

You can start this server on the command line with node. Make sure `websocket-example.js` is in the same directory (or installed as a module).

```
> node echo.js
```

If you then connect a WebSocket to this echo server from your browser, you will see that every message you send from your client is echoed back by the server.

▓ **Note**   When your server listens on localhost, the browser must be on the same machine. You can also try this out with the Echo client example from Chapter 2.

Building a Remote JavaScript Console

One of the best aspects of JavaScript is how amenable it is to interactive development. Consoles like those built into the Chrome Developer Tools and Firebug are one of the reasons JavaScript development can be so productive. A console, also called a REPL for "Real Eval Print Loop," lets you enter an expression and see the result. We'll take advantage of the Node.js repl module and add a custom eval() function. By adding WebSocket, we can remotely control a web application over the Internet! With this WebSocket-powered console, we will be able to remotely evaluate expressions from a command-line interface. Even better, we can enter one expression and see the results of evaluating that expression for every client concurrently connected.

In this example, you'll use the same server shown in Listing 3-6, then build two small snippets: one that acts as a remote control and one that acts as the object you control. Figure 3-8 shows what you'll build in the next example.

Figure 3-8. *Remote JavaScript console*

Before you build this example, ensure you've built the example in Listing 3-6. If you've also built the Echo Server piece (Listing 3-7), you'll need to shut down the Echo Server before testing the ensuing code snippets. Listing 3-8 contains the JavaScript code for the remote control.

Listing 3-8. websocket-repl.js

```
var websocket = require("./websocket-example");
var repl = require("repl");

var connections = Object.create(null);

var remoteMultiEval = function(cmd, context, filename, callback) {
    for (var c in connections) {
    connections[c].send(cmd);
    }
    callback(null, "(result pending)");
}

websocket.listen(9999, "localhost", function(conn) {
    conn.id = Math.random().toString().substr(2);
    connections[conn.id] = conn;
    console.log("new connection: " + conn.id);

    conn.on("data", function(opcode, data) {
    console.log("\t" + conn.id + ":\t" + data);
    });
    conn.on("close", function() {
```

```
    // remove connection
    delete connections[conn.id];
    });
});

repl.start({"eval": remoteMultiEval});
```

We will also need a simple web page to control. The script on this page simply opens a WebSocket to our control server, evaluates any message it receives, and responds with the result. The client also logs incoming expressions to the JavaScript console. You will see these expressions if you open your browser's developer tools. Listing 3-9 shows the web page containing the script.

Listing 3-9. repl-client.html

```
<!doctype html>
<title>WebSocket REPL Client</title>
<meta charset="utf-8">
<script>
var url = "ws://localhost:9999/repl";
var ws = new WebSocket(url);
ws.onmessage = function(e) {
    console.log("command: ", e.data);
    try {
        var result = eval(e.data);
        ws.send(result.toString());
    } catch (err) {
        ws.send(err.toString());
    }
}
</script>
```

Now if you run node `websocket-repl.js`, you will see an interactive interpreter. If you load `repl-client.html` in a couple of browsers, you will see that each browser evaluates your commands. Listing 3-10 shows the output for two expressions, navigator.userAgent and 5+5.

Listing 3-10. Expression Output from the Console

```
> new connection: 5206121257506311
new connection: 6689629901666194
navigator.userAgent
'(result pending)'
>     5206121257506311:    Mozilla/5.0 (X11; Ubuntu; Linux x86_64; rv:13.0)
Gecko/20100101 Firefox/13.0.1
    6689629901666194:    Mozilla/5.0 (X11; Linux x86_64) AppleWebKit/537.1
(KHTML, like Gecko) Chrome/21.0.1180.15 Safari/537.1
5+5
```

59

```
'(result pending)'
>      6689629901666194:    10
    5206121257506311:    10
```

Suggested Extensions

The remote JavaScript console is a good starting point for some interesting projects. Here are a couple ways to extend this example:

- Create an HTML5 user interface for the remote control console. Use a WebSocket to communicate between the user interface and the controlling server. Consider how using a socket simplifies sending pipelined commands and receiving delayed responses compared to a communication strategy like HTTP with AJAX.

- Once you've read Chapter 5, modify the remote control server to use STOMP. You could broadcast commands to every connected browser session using a topic and receive replies on a queue. Consider how to mix in new functionality such as a remote control service to a message driven application.

Summary

In this chapter, we explored a brief history of the Internet and protocols and why the WebSocket Protocol was created. We examined the WebSocket Protocol in detail, including the wire traffic, the opening and closing handshakes, and the framing format. We used Node.js to build an example WebSocket server powering a simple echo demo and a remote control console. While this chapter provides a good overview of the WebSocket Protocol, you can read the full protocol specification here: `http://tools.ietf.org/html/rfc6455`.

In the next chapters, we will use higher-level protocols on top of WebSocket to build feature-rich, real-time applications.

■ ■ ■

CHAPTER 4

Building Instant Messaging and Chat over WebSocket with XMPP

Chat is a great example of an Internet application that has become more difficult to build in an HTTP-only world. Chat and instant messaging applications are inherently asynchronous: either party can send a message at will without requiring a specific request or response. These applications are excellent use cases for WebSocket as they benefit hugely from reduced latency. When chatting with your friends and colleagues, you want as little delay as possible in order to have natural conversations. After all, if there were lots of lag, it would hardly be instant messaging.

Instant messaging is a perfect fit for WebSocket; chat applications are common demos and examples of this technology. Most common examples use simplistic custom messages instead of a standard protocol. In this chapter, we delve much deeper than these basic demos, using a mature protocol to tap into a wealth of different server implementations, powerful features, and proven scalability and extensibility.

First, we explore layering protocols with WebSocket and some of the key choices you need to make before building an application that uses a higher-level protocol over WebSocket. In this example, we use XMPP, which stands for eXtensible Messaging and Presence Protocol, and is a standard that is widely used in instant messaging applications. We take advantage of this protocol for communication by using it on top of a WebSocket transport layer. In our example, we step through connecting a web application to the Jabber Instant Messaging (IM) network using XMPP over WebSocket, including adding the ability to indicate user's status and online presence.

Layered Protocols

In Chapter 3, we discussed simple demonstrations of the WebSocket Protocol that involve sending and receiving messages directly on the WebSocket layer. Our remote control console example demonstrated that it is possible to use WebSocket to build simple applications involving bidirectional communication. Imagine extending simple demos like the remote control to build more full-featured applications like chat clients and servers. One of the great things about WebSocket is that you can layer other protocols on top of WebSocket to extend your applications over the Web. Let's take a look at layering a protocol over WebSocket.

Figure 4-1 shows a typical layering of Internet application layer protocols over TCP. An application uses a protocol like XMPP or STOMP (Simple Text Oriented Messaging Protocol, which we discuss in Chapter 5) to communicate between clients and servers. XMPP and STOMP, in turn, are communicated over TCP. When using encrypted

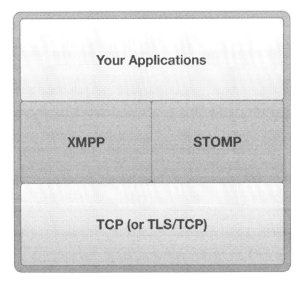

Figure 4-1. *Internet application layer diagram*

communication, the application layer protocols are on top of TLS (or SSL), which in turn is layered above TCP.

The WebSocket view of the world is much the same. Figure 4-2 shows a similar diagram with WebSocket inserted as an additional layer between the application layer protocols and TCP. XMPP and STOMP are layered on top of WebSocket, which is layered on top of TCP. In the encrypted case, secure WebSocket communication using the wss:// scheme is performed over a TLS connection. The WebSocket transport layer is a relatively thin layer that enables web applications to establish full duplex network connections. The WebSocket layer can be treated much the same as the TCP layer in Figure 4-1 and used for all of the same protocols.

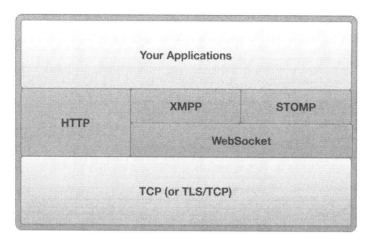

Figure 4-2. *Web application layer diagram*

Figure 4-2 includes HTTP for two reasons. One, it illustrates that HTTP exists as an application layer protocol on top of TCP that can be used directly in web applications. AJAX applications use HTTP as their primary or only protocol for all network interaction. Second, Figure 4-2 shows that applications using WebSocket do not need to completely ignore HTTP. Static resources are almost always loaded over HTTP. For instance, the HTML, JavaScript, and CSS making up your user interfaces can still be served over HTTP even when you choose to use WebSocket for communication. As such, in your application protocols stack, you might use both HTTP and WebSocket over TLS and TCP.

WebSocket really shines when used as a transport layer for standard application-level protocols. In doing so, you can reap the amazing benefits of a standard protocol along with the power of WebSocket. Let's take a look at some of these benefits by examining the widely used standard chat protocol, XMPP.

XMPP: A Streaming Mile of XML

Chances are high that you have read and written your fair share of XML (eXtensible Markup Language). XML is part of a long heritage of markup languages based on angle brackets stretching back several decades through SGML, HTML, and their ancestors. The World Wide Web Consortium (W3C) publishes its syntax and many web technologies use it. In fact, prior to HTML5, XHTML was the ordained successor to HTML4. The X in XML stands for eXtensible, and XMPP makes use of the extensibility it affords. Extending XMPP means using XML's extension mechanism to create namespaces, which are called XEPs (XMPP Extension Protocols). There is a large repository of XEPs at http://xmpp.org.

XML is a format for documents; XMPP is a protocol. So, how does XMPP use document syntax for real-time communication? One way to accomplish this is to send each message in a discrete document. However, this method would be unnecessarily verbose and wasteful. Another way is to treat the conversation as one long document that grows as time passes and messages are transmitted, which is how XMPP approaches the document syntax. Each direction of the bidirectional conversation that takes place during an XMPP connection is represented by a streaming XML document that ends when the connection terminates. The root node of that streaming document is a `<stream/>` element. The top-level children of the stream are the individual data units of the protocol, called *stanzas*. A typical stanza might look something like Listing 4-1, with whitespace removed to save bandwidth.

Listing 4-1. XMPP Stanza

```
<message type="chat" to="desktopuser@localhost">
<body>
  I like chatting. I also like angle brackets.
</body>
</message>
```

Standardization

You can use XMPP over WebSocket (XMPP/WS) today, although there is no standard for doing so. There is a draft specification at the IETF that may, after work and time, someday inspire a standard. There are also several implementations of XMPP/WS, some of them more experimental than others.

A standard for XMPP over WebSocket will let independent server and client implementations interoperate with a higher probability of success and will nail down all of the choices for binding XMPP communication to the WebSocket transport layer. These choices include options for each semantic difference between WebSocket and TCP and how to make use of message boundaries and opcodes, as discussed in Chapter 3. A standard will also define a stable subprotocol name for the protocol header in the WebSocket handshake that XMPP over WebSocket clients and servers will recognize. In the experimental stage, software you find or create to use XMPP over WebSocket may vary on some of these choices. Each variation is an opportunity for incompatibility between clients and servers that expect specific behavior.

While the benefits of standardization are numerous, we don't need to wait for a fully baked standard to build a cool application. We can select one client and one server that we know work well together. For example, the ejabberd-websockets module bundles a JavaScript client library that implements the draft proposal for XMPP over WebSocket. Alternatively, Kaazing WebSocket Gateway is a gateway (server) and incorporates a suite of compatible clients.

Choosing a Connectivity Strategy

There are two ways to connect to an XMPP server with WebSocket: modify the XMPP server to accept WebSocket connections or use a proxy server. While you can enable your XMPP server to accept XMPP over WebSocket, doing so requires an update to the server, which may not be possible if you do not control the server operations. Such is the case with public XMPP endpoints like `talk.google.com` and `chat.facebook.com`. In these cases, you need to create your own module according to the specification at http://tools.ietf.org/html/draft-moffitt-xmpp-over-websocket-01. Alternatively, at the time of the writing of this book, there are a few experimental modules: ejabberd-websockets and Openfire's module with WebSocket support. Figure 4-3 illustrates a client connecting to a WebSocket-enabled XMPP server.

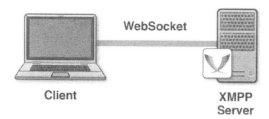

Figure 4-3. *Connecting to a WebSocket-aware XMPP server*

The second approach is to use a proxy server that accepts WebSocket connections from clients and makes corresponding TCP connections to back-end servers. In this case, the back-end servers are standard XMPP servers that accept XMPP over TCP connections. XmppClient in the Kaazing WebSocket Gateway takes this gateway approach. Here, applications can connect through Kaazing's gateway to any XMPP server, even servers that have no explicit support for WebSocket. Figure 4-4 shows an example of a WebSocket gateway server accepting WebSocket connections and making corresponding TCP connections to a back-end XMPP server.

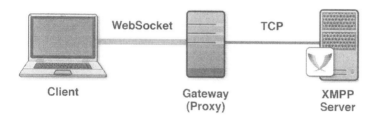

Figure 4-4. *Connecting to an XMPP server through a WebSocket proxy*

Stanza-to-Message Alignment

When choosing your connectivity strategy, it is important to understand how WebSocket messages (which typically comprise a single WebSocket frame) are aligned to XMPP stanzas, as the two approaches differ. In the case of WebSocket-aware XMPP servers, stanzas are mapped one-to-one onto WebSocket messages. Each WebSocket message contains exactly one stanza, and there can be no overlap or fragmentation. The draft XMPP for WebSocket subprotocol specifies this alignment. Stanza-to-message alignment is not necessary in the gateway scenario, because it is relaying WebSocket to TCP and vice versa. TCP does not have message boundaries, so the TCP stream might be split arbitrarily into WebSocket messages. In the gateway case, however, the client must be capable of defragmenting characters into stanzas by understanding streaming XML. Figure 4-5 shows the stanza-to-message alignment as described in the XMPP over WebSocket subprotocol draft proposal. See Chapter 2 and Chapter 3 for discussions about registering WebSocket subprotocol drafts.

Figure 4-5. *Stanza-to-message alignment (XMPP over WebSocket subprotocol draft proposal)*

This figure shows how WebSocket messages are aligned to XMPP stanzas in the case where an XMPP server can directly communicate over WebSocket to a client.

Figure 4-6 shows an example where the stanza is not aligned to the message. This figure shows how WebSocket messages do not need to be aligned to stanzas where a proxy server accepts WebSocket connections and connects to the back-end XMPP server over TCP.

Figure 4-6. *No stanza-to-message alignment (WebSocket to TCP proxy)*

Federation

Many IM networks are walled gardens. Users with accounts on a particular network can only chat among themselves. Conversely, Jabber (http://www.jabber.org) is federated, which means users on independently operated servers can communicate if the servers cooperate. The Jabber network comprises thousands of servers on different domains and millions of users. Configuring a server for federation is beyond the scope of this book. Here, we focus on connecting clients to a single server. You can later connect your server to the larger federated world.

Building a Chat and Instant Messaging Application over WebSocket

Now that we've walked through some of the important concepts behind using XMPP over WebSocket, let's take a look at a working example and delve into the more practical details. Here, we'll use a WebSocket-enabled XMPP server and build a typical chat application that communicates with the server using XMPP over WebSocket.

Using a WebSocket-Enabled XMPP Server

To build and run the example chat application for this chapter, you will need a WebSocket-enabled XMPP chat server that is compatible with a client library. As we mentioned, as of the writing of this book, there are a few options, including ejabberd-websockets, an Openfire module, and a proxy called node-xmpp-bosh that understands the WebSocket Protocol, an open source project built by Dhruv Matan. Because of the experimental nature of these modules, your mileage may vary. However, these modules are being rapidly developed, and you'll likely have numerous solid options by the publication (or your reading) of this book.

▓ **Note**   For the purposes of this bleeding-edge example, we've chosen Strophe.js for the client library. To build this example yourself, choose a WebSocket-enabled XMPP server (or update your own XMPP server) and ensure that it is compatible with Strophe.js. Alternatively, as previously mentioned, to build (or even follow) the examples in this book, you can use the virtual machine (VM) we've created that contains all the code, libraries, and servers we use in our examples. Refer to Appendix B for instructions on how to download, install, and start the VM. Due to the experimental nature of the technologies used in this chapter and for learning purposes, we strongly recommend you use the VM we've provided.

Setting Up Test Users

To test your chat application, you need a messaging network with at least two users to demonstrate interaction. To that end, create a pair of users on the WebSocket-enabled chat server. Then, you can use these test users to chat back and forth using the application you'll build in this chapter.

To ensure your server is correctly configured, try connecting two desktop XMPP clients. For example, you can install any two of the following clients: Pidgin, Psi, Spark, Adium, or iChat. You can find lots more at http://xmpp.org. Chances are, you already have one or two of them installed. In the first chat client, you should see the online status of the second user. Likewise, you should see the status of the first user in the second client. Leave one of these users logged in so that you can test your WebSocket chat application as you develop it.

The Client Library: Strophe.js

To enable your chat application to communicate with your chat server using XMPP over WebSocket, you need a client library that enables the client to interact with XMPP. In this example, we use Strophe.js, which is an open-source XMPP client library for JavaScript that can run in web browsers. Strophe.js provides a low-level API for interacting with XMPP, and includes functions for constructing, sending, and receiving stanzas. To build higher-level abstractions like chat clients, you'll need some knowledge of XMPP. However, Strophe.js is naturally extensible and gives precise control to developers using the library.

At the time of writing this book, the stable branch of Strophe.js uses a communication layer called BOSH. BOSH, specified in the XEP-0124 extension, stands for Bidirectional-streams over Synchronous HTTP. It is an XMPP-specific way of achieving bidirectional communication over half-duplex HTTP similar to the Comet techniques mentioned in Chapter 1. BOSH is older than WebSocket, and was developed out of similar needs to address the limitations of HTTP.

WEBSOCKET, NOT BOSH

The ejabberd-websocket README calls XMPP over WebSocket "a more elegant, modern and faster replacement to Bosh." Certainly, now that WebSocket has been standardized and is nearing ubiquitous deployment, Comet-like communication techniques are quickly becoming obsolete.

See Chapter 8 for a discussion of WebSocket emulation, which talks about how to use WebSocket with technologies that do not have native support.

Connecting and Getting Started

Before you start chatting, you need to connect your client to your XMPP/WS server. In this step, we will establish a connection from an HTML5 client application running in a web browser to a WebSocket-enabled XMPP server. The socket, once connected, will send XMPP stanzas back and forth between the client and the server for the duration of the session.

To get started, create a new file called `chat.html`, shown in Listing 4-2. The HTML portion of the application is just a bare-bones page including the Strophe.js library and the JavaScript comprising the chat application.

Listing 4-2. chat.html

```
<!DOCTYPE html>
<title>WebSocket Chat with XMPP</title>
<meta charset="UTF-8">
<link rel="stylesheet" href="chat.css">
<h1>WebSocket Chat with XMPP</h1>
```

```html
<!-- connect -->
<div class="panel">
    <input type="text" id="username" placeholder="username">
    <input type="password" id="password" placeholder="password">
    <button id="connectButton">Connect</button>
</div>

<div id="presenceArea" class="panel"></div>
<div id="chatArea" class="panel"></div>
<div id="output"></div>

<!-- scripts -->
<script src="strophe.js"></script>
<script src="chat_app.js"></script>
```

We will link this HTML document with a tiny CSS file that adds a little bit of style to the user interface, shown in Listing 4-3.

Listing 4-3. chat.css

```css
body {
 font-family: sans-serif;
}

#output {
  border: 2px solid black;
  border-radius: 8px;
  width: 500px;
}
    #output div {
      padding: 10px;
    }
    #output div:nth-child(even) {
      background-color: #ccc;
    }

panel {
 display: block;
 padding: 20px;
 border: 1px solid #ccc;
}
```

We will start with a minimal version of chat_app.js and add to it as we expand the functionality of this example. To begin, the script will simply connect to the XMPP server with Strophe.js and log its connection status. It also uses two input values: a username and a password. These values are used to authenticate the user when establishing the connection.

69

Listing 4-4. Initial Version of chat_app.js

```
// Log messages to the output area
var output = document.getElementById("output");
function log(message) {
    var line = document.createElement("div");
    line.textContent = message;
    output.appendChild(line);
}

function connectHandler(cond) {
 if (cond == Strophe.Status.CONNECTED) {
    log("connected");
    connection.send($pres());
    }
}

var url = "ws://localhost:5280/";
var connection = null;

var connectButton = document.getElementById("connectButton");
connectButton.onclick = function() {
    var username = document.getElementById("username").value;
    var password = document.getElementById("password").value;
connection = new Strophe.Connection(
    {proto: new Strophe.Websocket(url)});
    connection.connect(username, password, connectHandler);
}
```

Be aware that this example requires the user to enter his or her credentials. In production, it is very important to make sure that credentials are not sent across the network unencrypted. Actually, it is far better to not send credentials across the network at all. See Chapter 7 for information about using encryption and authentication for WebSocket. If your chat application is part of a larger suite of web applications, you'll likely want to use a single sign-on mechanism, especially if you are building a chat widget for a larger site or if your users authenticate with external credentials.

If everything goes according to plan, you should see "connected" logged onto the page. If so, you have successfully logged a user into a chat server using XMPP over WebSocket. You should see the connected user has come online in the roster UI of the other XMPP client that you left connected earlier (see Figure 4-7).

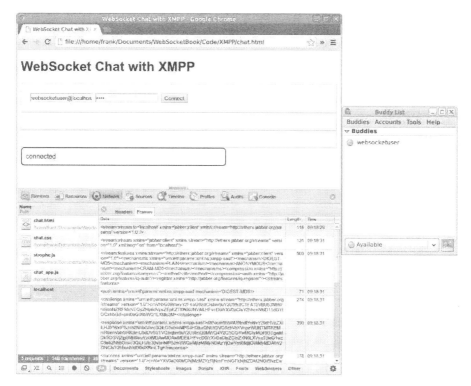

Figure 4-7. *Logging in from chat.html and appearing online in Pidgin. Each WebSocket message displayed in the developer tools contains an XMPP stanza*

■ **Note**   The $pres()$ function call in the connect handler is necessary to indicate that the user has logged online. These presence updates can convey more details, as we will see in the next section.

Presence and Status

Now that we know we can connect a user, let's take a look at tracking user presence and status. The way the web user appeared to be online in the contact list of the desktop user is due to the presence features of XMPP. Even when you are not chatting, presence information is constantly pushed out from the server. You may receive presence updates when your contacts sign online, become idle, or change their status text.

In XMPP, each user has a presence. The presence has an availability value, represented by a *show* tag, and a *status message*. To change this presence information, send a presence stanza, as shown in Listing 4-5:

Listing 4-5. Presence Stanza Example

```
<presence>
<show>chat</show>
   <status>Having a lot of fun with WebSocket</status>
</presence>
```

Let's add a way for the user to change their status to chat_app.js (see Listing 4-6). First, we can append some basic form controls to set the online/offline portion of the status, called "show" in XMPP parlance. These controls will display as a dropdown menu with the four choices for availability. The values in the dropdown menu have short specified names like "dnd" for "do not disturb." We will also give these human readable labels like "Away" and "Busy."

Listing 4-6. Presence Update UI

```
// Create presence update UI
var presenceArea = document.getElementById("presenceArea");
var sel = document.createElement("select");
var availabilities = ["away", "chat", "dnd", "xa"];
var labels = ["Away", "Available", "Busy", "Gone"];
for (var i=0; i<availabilities.length; i++) {
    var option = document.createElement("option");
    option.value = availabilities[i];
    option.text = labels[i];
    sel.add(option);
}
presenceArea.appendChild(sel);
```

The status text is free form, so we will use an input element, as shown in Listing 4-7.

Listing 4-7. Input Element for Status Text

```
var statusInput = document.createElement("input");
statusInput.setAttribute("placeholder", "status");
presenceArea.appendChild(statusInput);
```

Finally, we'll add a button that causes the update to be sent out to the server (see Listing 4-8). The $pres function builds a presence stanza. To update the status of the connected user, the presence stanza contains two child nodes: show and status. Try this out, and notice that the desktop client reflects the web user's status practically instantaneously. Figure 4-8 illustrates the example so far.

Listing 4-8. Button Event to Send the Update

```
var statusButton = document.createElement("button");
statusButton.onclick = function() {
    var pres = $pres()
    .c("show").t("away").up()
    .c("status").t(statusInput.value);
    connection.send(pres)
}
presenceArea.appendChild(statusButton);
```

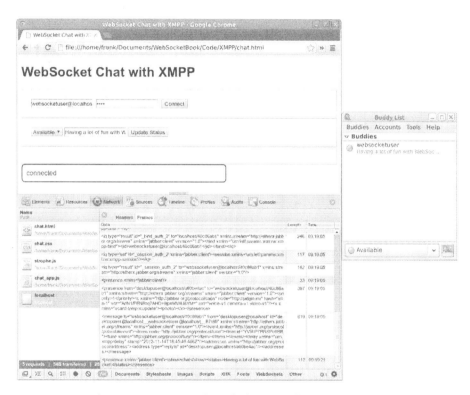

Figure 4-8. *Updating presence status from the browser. The most recent WebSocket message sent by the client contains a presence stanza.message by client*

To see other users' presence updates in our web application, we need to understand incoming presence stanzas. In this simplified example, these presence updates will just be logged as text. Listing 4-9 shows how to do this in chat_app.js. In a full-fledged chat application, the presence updates are usually updated next to the chat conversation.

Listing 4-9. Handling Presence Updates

```
function presenceHandler(presence) {
    var from = presence.getAttribute("from");
    var show = "";
    var status = "";
    Strophe.forEachChild(presence, "show", function(elem) {
        show = elem.textContent;
    });
Strophe.forEachChild(presence, "status", function(elem) {
    status = elem.textContent;
});

//
    if (show || status){
        log("[presence] " + from + ":" + status + " " + show);
    }

// indicate that this handler should be called repeatedly
    return true;
}
```

To handle presence updates with this function, we register the handler with the connection object (see Listing 4-10). This call to addHandler() will associate the presenceHandler() function with every presence stanza.

Listing 4-10. Registering the Presence Handler

```
connection.addHandler(presenceHandler, null, "presence", null);
```

Figure 4-9 shows that as websocketuser updates his presence status using the desktop client to "Gone fishing – Do Not Disturb," the browser client displays it right away.

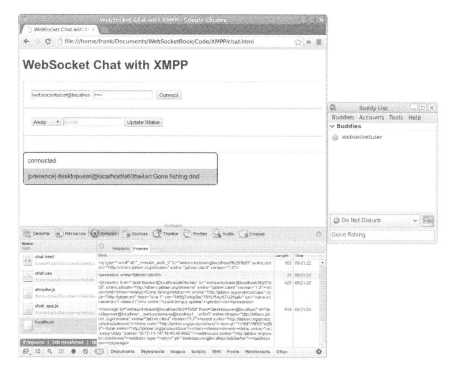

Figure 4-9. *Observing presence changes in the browser*

Exchanging Chat Messages

Here, we get to the core of any IM application: chat messages. Chat messages are
represented as message stanzas with the type attribute set to chat. The Strophe.js
connection API has an addHandler() function that lets us listen for incoming message
stanzas matching that type, as shown in Listing 4-11.

Listing 4-11. Listening for Incoming "Chat" Message Stanzas

```
function messageHandler(message) {
    var from = message.getAttribute("from");
    var body = "";
    Strophe.forEachChild(message, "body", function(elem) {
        body = elem.textContent;
});

// Log message if body was present
if (body) {
    log(from + ": " + body);
}
```

```
// Indicate that this handler should be called repeatedly
   return true;
}
```

We also need to associate this handler with the connection after connecting, as shown in Listing 4-12.

Listing 4-12. Associating the addHandler with the Connection

```
connection.addHandler(messageHandler, null, "message", "chat");
```

Now, try sending a message from one of your chat clients, like Pidgin, to the web user. The message handler function should be called with a message stanza. Figure 4-10 illustrates a chat message exchange.

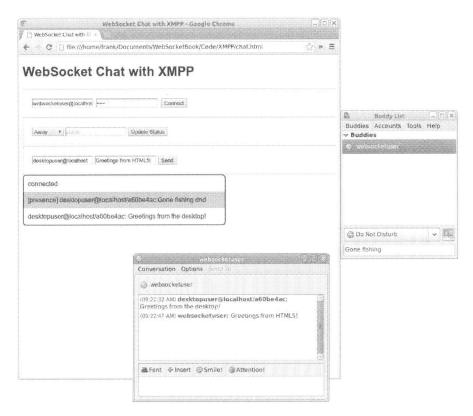

Figure 4-10. Chatting between Pidgin and chat.html

To send a message back to the web user, you need to send a message stanza to the server. This message stanza must have a type attribute of "chat" and a body element containing the actual chat text, as shown in Listing 4-13.

Listing 4-13. Sending a Message Stanza to the Server

```
<message type="chat" to="desktopuser@localhost">
<body>
   I like chatting. I also like angle brackets.
</body>
</message>
```

To build this message with Strophe.js, use the $msg builder function. Create a message stanza with the *type* attribute set to chat and the *to* attribute set to the user with whom you want to chat. The other user should receive the message shortly after you send the message on the connection. Listing 4-14 shows an example of this message stanza.

Listing 4-14. Building a Message with Strophe.js

```
// Create chat UI
var chatArea = document.getElementById("chatArea");
var toJid = document.createElement("input");
toJid.setAttribute("placeholder", "user@server");
chatArea.appendChild(toJid);

var chatBody = document.createElement("input");
chatBody.setAttribute("placeholder", "chat body");
chatArea.appendChild(chatBody);

var sendButton = document.createElement("button");
sendButton.textContent = "Send";
sendButton.onclick = function() {
   var message = $msg({to: toJid.value, type:"chat"})
  .c("body").t(chatBody.value);
 connection.send(message);
}
chatArea.appendChild(sendButton);
```

And now, you're chatting. Of course, you can chat between web clients, desktop clients, or a combination of the two. This chat application is a great example of HTML5 and WebSocket enabling desktop-class experiences in the web browser through integration with standard network protocols. This web application is a true peer of the desktop client. They are both first-class participants in the same network, because they understand the same application level protocol. And yes, XMPP is a standard protocol, even if this particular layering onto WebSocket is not yet standardized. It retains nearly all of the benefits of XMPP over TCP, even as a draft.

Conversations between any number of web and desktop clients are possible. The same users can connect from either client. In Figure 4-11, both users are using the web client.

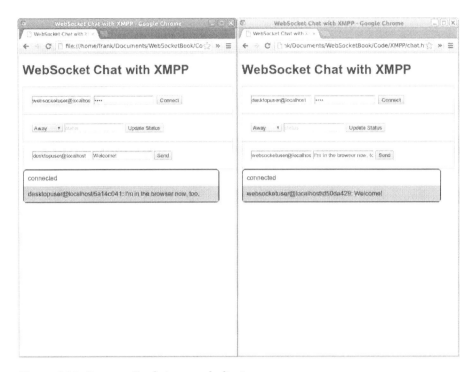

Figure 4-11. *Conversation between web clients*

Pings and Pongs

Depending on your server configuration, this application might automatically disconnect after a period of time. The disconnection is probably because the server sent a ping and the client didn't promptly respond with a pong. Pings and pongs are used in XMPP for the same purpose they are used in WebSocket: to keep connections alive and to check the health of a connection. Pings and pongs use *iq* stanzas. In XMPP, "iq" stands for info/ query and is a way of performing request/response queries on top of the asynchronous connection. A ping looks like Listing 4-15.

Listing 4-15. XMPP Server ping

```
<iq type="get" id="86-14" from="localhost"
   to="websocketuser@localhost/cc9fd219" >
   <ping xmlns="urn:xmpp:ping"/>
</iq>
```

The server will expect a response in the form of an *iq* result with the matching ID (see Listing 4-16).

Listing 4-16. Setting the Client Response

```
<iq type="result" id="86-14" to="localhost"
    from "websocketuser@localhost/cc9fd219" />
```

To handle pings in Strophe.js, we need to register a function to handle all iq stanzas with the `urn:xmpp:ping` namespace and `type="get"` (see Listing 4-17). As in the previous steps, we do this by registering a handler on the connection object. The handler code builds the appropriate response and sends it back to the server.

Listing 4-17. Registering a Handler for iq Stanzas

```
function pingHandler(ping) {
    var pingId = ping.getAttribute("id");
    var from = ping.getAttribute("from");
    var to = ping.getAttribute("to");
    var pong = $iq({type: "result", "to": from, id: pingId, "from": to});
    connection.send(pong);

// Indicate that this handler should be called repeatedly
    return true;
}
```

Listing 4-18 shows how the handler is registered.

Listing 4-18. Registered addHandler

```
connection.addHandler(pingHandler, "urn:xmpp:ping", "iq", "get");
```

Completed Chat Application

Listing 4-19 shows the finished, end-to-end chat application, complete with pings and pongs.

Listing 4-19. Final Version of chat_app.js

```
// Log messages to the output area
var output = document.getElementById("output");
function log(message) {
    var line = document.createElement("div");
    line.textContent = message;
    output.appendChild(line);
}

function connectHandler(cond) {
    if (cond == Strophe.Status.CONNECTED) {
        log("connected");
        connection.send($pres());
    }
}
```

```
var url = "ws://localhost:5280/";
var connection = null;

var connectButton = document.getElementById("connectButton");
connectButton.onclick = function() {
    var username = document.getElementById("username").value;
    var password = document.getElementById("password").value;
    connection = new Strophe.Connection({proto: new Strophe.Websocket(url)});
    connection.connect(username, password, connectHandler);

// Set up handlers
    connection.addHandler(messageHandler, null, "message", "chat");
    connection.addHandler(presenceHandler, null, "presence", null);
    connection.addHandler(pingHandler, "urn:xmpp:ping", "iq", "get");
}

// Create presence update UI
var presenceArea = document.getElementById("presenceArea");
var sel = document.createElement("select");
var availabilities = ["away", "chat", "dnd", "xa"];
var labels = ["Away", "Available", "Busy", "Gone"];
for (var i=0; i<availabilities.length; i++) {
    var option = document.createElement("option");
    option.value = availabilities[i];
    option.text = labels[i];
    sel.add(option);
}
presenceArea.appendChild(sel);

var statusInput = document.createElement("input");
statusInput.setAttribute("placeholder", "status");
presenceArea.appendChild(statusInput);

var statusButton = document.createElement("button");
statusButton.textContent = "Update Status";
statusButton.onclick = function() {
    var pres = $pres();
        c("show").t(sel.value).up();
        c("status").t(statusInput.value);
    connection.send(pres);
}
presenceArea.appendChild(statusButton);
function presenceHandler(presence) {
    var from = presence.getAttribute("from");
    var show = "";
    var status = "";
```

```
Strophe.forEachChild(presence, "show", function(elem) {
   show = elem.textContent;
});

Strophe.forEachChild(presence, "status", function(elem) {
   status = elem.textContent;
});

if (show || status){
   log("[presence] " + from + ":" + status + " " + show);
}

// Indicate that this handler should be called repeatedly
   return true;
}

// Create chat UI
var chatArea = document.getElementById("chatArea");
var toJid = document.createElement("input");
toJid.setAttribute("placeholder", "user@server");
chatArea.appendChild(toJid);

var chatBody = document.createElement("input");
chatBody.setAttribute("placeholder", "chat body");
chatArea.appendChild(chatBody);

var sendButton = document.createElement("button");
sendButton.textContent = "Send";
sendButton.onclick = function() {
   var message = $msg({to: toJid.value, type:"chat"})
   .c("body").t(chatBody.value);
   connection.send(message);
}
chatArea.appendChild(sendButton);

function messageHandler(message) {
   var from = message.getAttribute("from");
   var body = "";
   Strophe.forEachChild(message, "body", function(elem) {
       body = elem.textContent;
});

// Log message if body was present
if (body) {
   log(from + ": " + body);
}
```

```
// Indicate that this handler should be called repeatedly
   return true;
}

function pingHandler(ping) {
   var pingId = ping.getAttribute("id");
   var from = ping.getAttribute("from");
   var to = ping.getAttribute("to");

   var pong = $iq({type: "result", "to": from, id: pingId, "from": to});
   connection.send(pong);

// Indicate that this handler should be called repeatedly
   return true;
}
```

Suggested Extensions

Now that we've built a basic browser-based chat application, you can take this example and do lots of other cool things to turn it into a full-fledged application.

Build a User Interface

Our example web page, chat.html, obviously does not have the most beautiful or usable user interface. Consider enhancing the UI of your chat client to incorporate more user-friendly features like tabbed conversations, automatic scrolling, and a visible contact list. Another benefit of building this as a web application is that you have many powerful tools for making a gorgeous and flexible design come to life with HTML, CSS, and JavaScript.

Use XMPP Extensions

XMPP has a rich extension ecosystem. There are hundreds of extension proposals or "XEPs" on http://xmpp.org. These range from functionality like avatars and group chat to VOIP session initialization.

XMPP can be a great way to add social features to web applications. The built-in support for contacts, presence, and chat provides a social core on top of which you can add collaboration, social notifications, and so on. Many extensions have this goal. These include XEPS for microblogging, commenting, avatars, and publishing personal event streams.

Connect to Google Talk

Google Talk, the chat service you may be familiar with from Gmail and Google+, is actually part of the Jabber IM network. There is a publicly accessible XMPP server listening on talk.google.com on port 5222. If you have a Google account, you can point any compatible XMPP client at that address and log in. To connect to Google Talk with your own web client, point a WebSocket proxy server at that address. That server requires encryption, so make sure the server is configured to make connections over TLS.

Summary

In this chapter, we explored how to layer protocols, specifically standard protocols, over WebSocket and how standard application layer protocols like XMPP may fit into a standard web architecture. We built a simple chat client that uses the widely used chat protocol, XMPP, over WebSocket. In doing so, we saw the power of using WebSocket as a transport layer along with this standard application layer protocol to connect a web application to an interactive network.

In the next chapter, we will use STOMP on top of WebSocket to build a feature-rich, real-time messaging application.

CHAPTER 5

Using Messaging over WebSocket with STOMP

In the previous chapter, we explored the concept of layering protocols over WebSocket and some of the key benefits of layering a standards-based protocol over WebSocket. Specifically, we looked at building a standard instant messaging and presence protocol, XMPP, over WebSocket. In this chapter, we examine how to use a messaging protocol with WebSocket.

Messaging is an architectural style characterized by sending asynchronous messages between independent components, allowing you to build loosely coupled systems. Messaging provides an abstraction layer for communication patterns, and thus is a very flexible and powerful way to write networked applications.

Key players in messaging are the message broker and the clients. The message broker accepts connections from the clients, handles messages coming from the clients, and sends messages to them. The broker can also handle responsibilities such as authentication, authorization, message encryption, reliable message delivery, message throttling, and fanout. When clients connect to the message broker, they can send messages to the broker, as well as receive messages sent by the broker to them. This model is called publish/subscribe, where the message broker publishes a number of messages and the client subscribes to all or, more commonly, a subset of the messages.

Messaging is widely used in enterprises as well to integrate disparate enterprise applications. Besides loosely coupling enterprise systems, enterprise messaging focuses on key enterprise requirements, including encryption, single sign-on, authorization, high availability, and scalability.

Similar to how we layered XMPP over WebSocket, you can also layer a publish/subscribe protocol over WebSocket. One example of a publish/subscribe (or, colloquially, pub/sub) protocol is STOMP (Simple or Streaming Text Oriented Messaging Protocol). Figure 5-1 shows a diagram of how STOMP over WebSocket relates to the layering of other protocols.

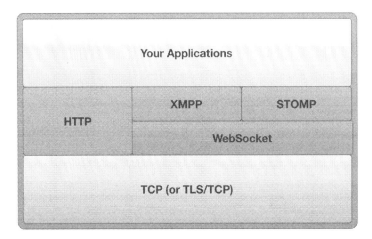

Figure 5-1. *Layering STOMP over WebSocket*

WebSocket is very well suited to a typical messaging architecture, where there may be a high volume of messages flowing from the message broker to the client at fast rates. For example, one typical use case for messaging is a client subscribing to foreign exchange or stock information; in this case, the messages (the exchange rate, the stock value, and so on) are very small but the client's receiving of the messages in real time and with low latency is crucial to the success of the application. Based on what you've hopefully learned in this book so far, you can see how WebSocket is a great fit for such applications.

In this chapter, we'll examine pub/sub models, a widely used protocol (STOMP), then walk through building your own pub/sub application—a game!—using STOMP over WebSocket. We'll use the popular open source message broker Apache ActiveMQ and explore some of the ways you can use STOMP with WebSocket in your own architecture.

░ **Note**   The *Text* portion of the STOMP definition signifies that the protocol is text oriented. Chapter 6, which focuses on the RFB protocol, describes how to use a binary-oriented protocol over WebSocket.

Overview of Publish and Subscribe Models

A common messaging pattern is the publish/subscribe pattern (pub/sub). In the pub/sub pattern, clients connect to a broker that dispatches messages. A client can publish messages to the broker and/or subscribe to one or more message feeds.

In the messaging world there are two frequently used message distribution techniques, as shown in Figure 5-2:

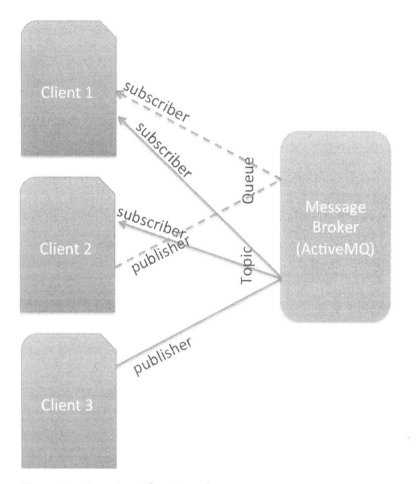

Figure 5-2. *Messaging with topics and queues*

- Queue: A distribution mechanism for delivering messages to a single consumer. Any number of clients (publishers) can publish messages to a queue, but every message is consumed by one and only one client (consumer).

- Topic: A distribution mechanism for delivering messages to multiple consumers. Any number of clients (publishers) can publish messages to a topic, and any number of clients (consumers) can consume them.

▩ **Note** Not every message broker uses topics and queues. In this chapter, though, we use Apache ActiveMQ, which does support topics and queues.

The more you use WebSocket, the more you may realize that the requirements for building WebSocket-powered applications resemble classic messaging concepts. For example, perhaps you want to extend the reach of your enterprise messaging protocols to the Web by distributing large quantities of messages to a large number of clients. Or, suppose you're building a collaborative application that requires your WebSocket clients to send and receive data to and from other WebSocket clients. These two examples illustrate messaging applications and WebSocket applications alike. As you will see in this chapter, the two technologies work well together and layering messaging over WebSocket enables you to build powerful messaging applications.

Messaging systems differ in how they integrate with clients. Some, like brokers that support STOMP, offer protocol-level interoperability. Anyone implementing a compatible protocol client can connect to those systems from any platform and language. Others offer APIs that are provided for some select platforms chosen by the system vendor.

The simplest open, widely used protocol for messaging is STOMP: Simple (or Streaming) Text Oriented Messaging Protocol. The most widely used messaging API in the enterprise is JMS: Java Message Service. Unlike STOMP, which promotes interoperability by defining a wire protocol, JMS is just an API. STOMP has been implemented for many different languages; because of its nature as an API, JMS is almost exclusively reigning in the Java world.

A newly standardized open messaging protocol is AMQP: Advanced Message Queuing Protocol. AMQP 1.0 became an OASIS standard in October 2012. Although AMQP was created with wide industry support, whether it can live up to the popularity and success of STOMP and JMS remains to be seen. To learn more about AMQP, see `http://amqp.org`.

In this chapter we walk through using STOMP over WebSocket (STOMP/WS). But if your interest is JMS or AMQP over WebSocket, there are vendors and projects that can offer you these capabilities. In addition, there are several proprietary pub/sub implementations over WebSocket: some are simple, some more sophisticated. See Appendix B for a list of current WebSocket servers that may have the support you need. The steps in this chapter will hopefully also help give you a general understanding of how pub/sub over WebSocket implementations work.

Introduction to STOMP

STOMP is an open protocol for messaging that was originally developed for use with Apache ActiveMQ and has spread widely to other systems. STOMP does not have topics or queues. STOMP messages are sent and received from destinations; the STOMP server decides how these destinations behave. This behavior is similar to HTTP, in that servers just have URLs, and it is up to the server to decide how to serve those URLs. In the example we build in this chapter, we use STOMP with ActiveMQ. ActiveMQ uses destination names to expose messaging features including topics and queues, temporary destinations, and hierarchical subscriptions.

There is a running joke about standards whose names include the word "simple": they are almost universally overcomplicated. Examples include SNMP (Simple Network Management Protocol), SOAP (Simple Object Access Protocol), and SMTP (Simple Mail Transfer Protocol). STOMP is a genuinely *simple* protocol: it is text oriented and resembles HTTP in its appearance. Each frame consists of a command, headers, and a body. STOMP message bodies can contain any text or binary data. Listing 5-1 shows an example SEND frame containing a text body. This example depicts a NULL terminated SEND frame, which sends a message to a destination named /topic/hello/world. The black square at the end of the message represents NULL, an unprintable character.

Listing 5-1. A NULL Terminated SEND Frame

```
SEND

destination: /topic/hello/world

content-type: text/plain

hello, world!

■
```

The content-length header communicates the size of the frame body. This header is optional. Messages without content-length headers end with NULL (0x00) bytes to mark the end of their body content. Messages terminated in that way cannot contain NULL bytes in the middle of their payload.

■ **Note**   The syntax of STOMP frames is handled by client and server software you can use in your applications, but if you would like to develop your own implementation, you can refer to the specification at http://stomp.github.com.

You can layer STOMP over WebSocket in the same manner as any TCP-level protocol, or align it such that each STOMP frame occupies exactly one WebSocket frame.

Getting Started with Web Messaging

Now that we've examined messaging concepts, as well as some of the great benefits WebSocket can bring to a messaging protocol like STOMP, let's build a working example of a messaging application that communicates messages via a message broker to a client, using STOMP over WebSocket.

In this example, we'll use a widely available open source message broker, Apache ActiveMQ, which supports WebSocket. We'll step through configuring ActiveMQ to accept WebSocket connections, allowing us to communicate using STOMP over WebSocket. ActiveMQ also conveniently includes out-of-the-box demos, which we'll use to walk through some of the concepts we've discussed. Then, we'll build our own STOMP/WS application. You can learn more about ActiveMQ at http://activemq.apache.org.

■ **Note** To build (or even follow) the examples in this book, you can choose to use the virtual machine (VM) we've created that contains all the code, libraries, and servers we use in our examples. Refer to Appendix B for instructions on how to download, install, and start the VM.

Setting Up a Message Broker

To get started, download the message broker from `http://activemq.apache.org/download.html`. At the time of writing this book, the most recent ActiveMQ version available is 5.7, supporting STOMP 1.1, but more recent versions should work just as well.

■ **Note** The ActiveMQ download is available in two flavors: one for Windows (`*.zip`), and one for the various Unix flavors: Linux, Unix, and Mac (`*.tar.gz`).

After downloading and extracting ActiveMQ, your directory structure should look similar to what's shown in Figure 5-3.

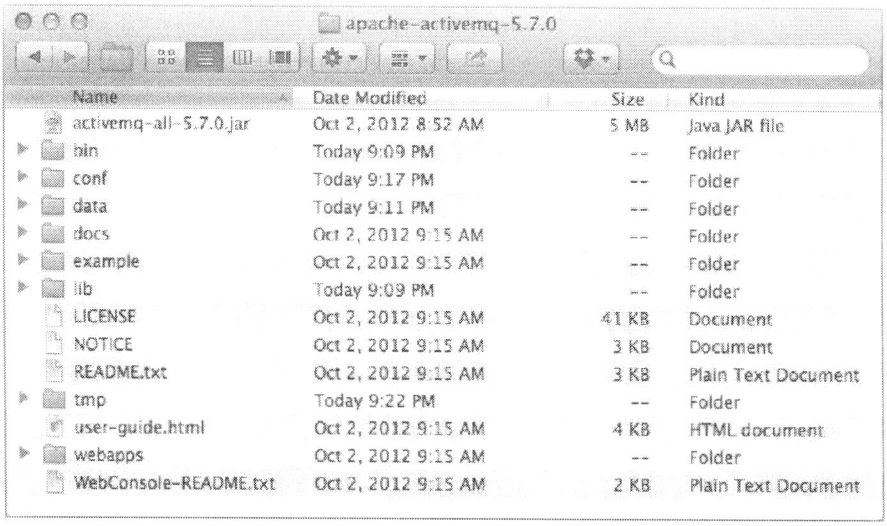

Name	Date Modified	Size	Kind
activemq-all-5.7.0.jar	Oct 2, 2012 8:52 AM	5 MB	Java JAR file
▶ bin	Today 9:09 PM	--	Folder
▶ conf	Today 9:17 PM	--	Folder
▶ data	Today 9:11 PM	--	Folder
▶ docs	Oct 2, 2012 9:15 AM	--	Folder
▶ example	Oct 2, 2012 9:15 AM	--	Folder
▶ lib	Today 9:09 PM	--	Folder
LICENSE	Oct 2, 2012 9:15 AM	41 KB	Document
NOTICE	Oct 2, 2012 9:15 AM	3 KB	Document
README.txt	Oct 2, 2012 9:15 AM	3 KB	Plain Text Document
▶ tmp	Today 9:22 PM	--	Folder
user-guide.html	Oct 2, 2012 9:15 AM	4 KB	HTML document
▶ webapps	Oct 2, 2012 9:15 AM	--	Folder
WebConsole-README.txt	Oct 2, 2012 9:15 AM	2 KB	Plain Text Document

Figure 5-3. *The ActiveMQ home directory after installation*

To start ActiveMQ, open a terminal and navigate to the `bin` directory in your ActiveMQ home, which is the directory where you extracted ActiveMQ. Run the command shown in Listing 5-2.

Listing 5-2. Starting Apache ActiveMQ

```
$> ./activemq console
```

After successfully starting up ActiveMQ, you can open a browser and navigate to the Welcome page at `http://0.0.0.0:8161`, as shown in Figure 5-4.

Figure 5-4. The Apache ActiveMQ Welcome Page

The Welcome page lists useful links. The first link, Manage ActiveMQ broker, takes you to the ActiveMQ management console, which we'll describe in more depth later. The second link, "See some Web demos" takes you to the launch page for the demos that ship with the product. Click the See some Web demos link, or simply append /demo to the URL: `http://0.0.0.0:8161/demo`.

The first demo in the list is the WebSocket example. In order for this demo to work, we need to configure the WebSocket transport that implements STOMP over it. In your terminal, stop ActiveMQ; for example, if you started it with the command in Listing 5-1, simply press Ctrl+C. Once you've stopped ActiveMQ, you can now configure the message broker to use WebSocket.

First, open the file `ActiveMQ_HOME/conf/activemq.xml` and search for the string `transportConnectors`. Below the openwire transport connector, add the snippet shown in Listing 5-3.

Listing 5-3. Declaring the WebSocket Connector

```
<transportConnectors>
    <transportConnector name="websocket" uri="ws://0.0.0.0:61614"/>
</transportConnectors>
```

Now, the transport connector section of your `activemq.xml` file should look similar to Listing 5-4 (newly added section highlighted).

Listing 5-4. activemq.xml Snippet with the WebSocket Connector

```
<!-- The transport connectors expose ActiveMQ over a given
     protocol to clients and other brokers. For more
     information, see:
     http://activemq.apache.org/configuring-transports.html -->
<transportConnectors>
    <transportConnector name="openwire" uri="tcp://0.0.0.0:61616"/>
</transportConnectors>
<transportConnectors>
    <transportConnector name="websocket" uri="ws://0.0.0.0:61614"/>
</transportConnectors>
```

Save the `activemq.xml` file and start ActiveMQ again, as shown in Listing 5-2. Confirm that the WebSocket connector has been started, by looking for the line shown in Listing 5-5 in the console.

Listing 5-5. Log Message Indicating that the WebSocket Connector has been Started

```
INFO | Connector websocket Started
```

Now, you're ready to start the WebSocket example that ships as part of ActiveMQ. Navigate to `http://0.0.0.0:8161/demo`, and click the WebSocket example link, or simply enter the direct URL in your browser's address bar: `http://0.0.0.0:8161/demo/websockets.html`.

Figure 5-5 shows the page that displays at this URL.

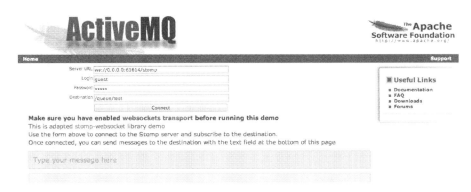

Figure 5-5. *The WebSocket Demo, which ships with Apache ActiveMQ*

■ **Note**   To troubleshoot the demo or learn more about configuring WebSocket with ActiveMQ, see the product's instructions at `http://activemq.apache.org/websockets.html`.

Seeing STOMP Concepts in Action

ActiveMQ's WebSocket demo illustrates some of the basic STOMP concepts we discussed earlier in this chapter and provides an easy way to see them in action before building the application ourselves. Let's take a look at how these concepts surface in this demo.

To get started, you must first connect to the server. When we updated the `activemq.xml` file, we set up the server URL at `ws://0.0.0.0:61614/stomp`. You can use this URL now. Then, you need to provide user credentials: a user name and a password. We will use guest both as the user name (labeled as Login in the sample), and as the password. Finally, you must provide a queue as a destination. By default it's called test. The `/queue` prefix indicates that this is a queue, and `/test` is the name of the queue. Feel free to change the latter part of the string, for example: `/queue/stompDemo`.

■ **Note**   For the demo to work, you just need to change the server URL. Be sure to use `0.0.0.0` instead of `localhost`. All the other fields are pre-populated for you, and you don't need to change them.

After you click Connect, your application displays, as shown in Figure 5-6.

Figure 5-6. *Running the Apache ActiveMQ WebSocket Demo*

In Figure 5-6, notice that the STOMP messages are logged. Let's take a closer look at these messages. First, the WebSocket connection is established, and a STOMP connection is opened with the credentials provided: guest/guest. A heartbeat message is then sent. After successfully creating the STOMP connection, the demo application subscribes to the stompDemo queue.

Now, open a second browser window (you can open a new window of the same browser or start a different browser) and provide the exact same connection data you used above. At this point, you can start sending messages back and forth between the browser windows.

Building a STOMP over WebSocket Application

Now that we've looked at a simple demo of a STOMP/WS application, let's try building one. Here, we step through building an application that allows users to play the popular hand game rock-paper-scissors, also known as "roshambo." If you're not familiar with the game, Wikipedia provides plenty of information about it: http://en.wikipedia.org/wiki/Rock-paper-scissors.

The Flow of the Game

Let's review the requirements and the flow of the game. The traditional way of playing the game requires participants to call their object (rock, paper, or scissors) at exactly the same time. To achieve this, the game is preceded by a "sync-up phase," after which the players shout their choice.

The beauty of playing the game in a browser is that users can be remote, which also means that this "sync-up phase" will work slightly differently. To imitate the "sync-up phase" in an online setting, we'll instead hide the players' selections from each other until both players have picked their object.

Here is an overview of how the browser-based game works between two players:

1. Player 1 (the player that moves first) selects an option (rock, paper, or scissors). Player 1's app displays this selection.

2. Player 2's (the slower player's) app receives Player 1's move (but does not display the selection) and indicates that Player 1 has made a selection.

3. Player 2 selects a move (rock, paper, or scissors).

4. Player 1's app receives and displays Player 2's selection.

5. Player 2's app displays the selections of both Player 1 and Player 2.

The challenge with building this application is whether we can make it run exclusively in the browser, without any back-end code or logic. How do we do this? With messaging and WebSocket, of course.

First, we must consider how the apps will communicate. For the purposes of this demonstration, we'll walk through building this game with two players, where the two applications communicate directly with each other. You'll recall from Figure 5-2 that we can use queues (which deliver messages to a single consumer), rather than topics (which distribute messages to multiple consumers).

To achieve our goals, and keep our application reasonably straightforward, we build the app with two queues, where Player 1's app publishes to one queue and Player 2's app consumes from the same queue. Player 2's app then publishes to a second queue and Player 1's app consumes messages from the second queue.

The queues will be identified by the players' names that we ask them to enter before starting the game.

Based on these requirements, let's walk through the players' interactions with the app. When the app starts, it waits for the players to enter their names, as shown in Figure 5-7.

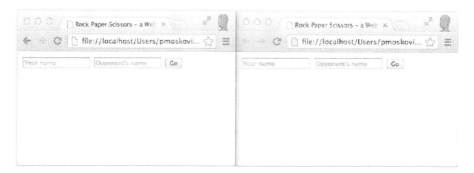

Figure 5-7. *Running the rock-paper-scissors application in two browser windows side-by-side*

The players enter their names and click the Go button, as shown in Figure 5-8.

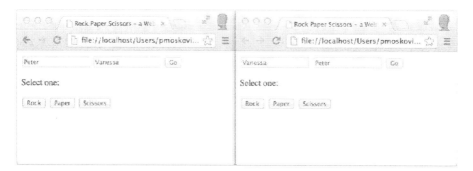

Figure 5-8. *Users entering their names in the rock-paper-scissors application*

Player 1 (Peter) makes a selection. This selection is reflected in the interface, as shown in Figure 5-9. On Player 2's (Vanessa's) screen, a message displays that indicates to the player that the opponent has made a selection: Your opponent is waiting for you. Make your move!

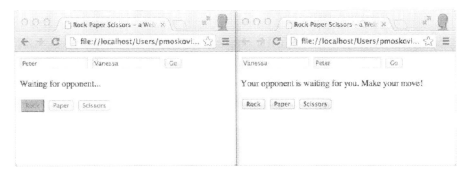

Figure 5-9. *Player 1 moves*

After the second player makes a selection, the results are displayed immediately to both players, as shown in Figure 5-10.

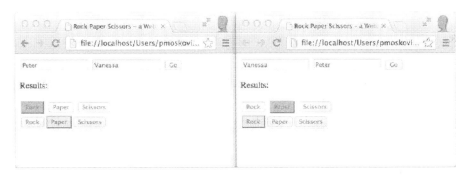

Figure 5-10. *Player 2 moves*

In a "real" rock-paper-scissors game, after each round you want to declare a winner. For the sake of keeping this demo simple and the source code focused, we do not include this feature.

Creating the Game

Our simple application consists of our own HTML and a JavaScript file, and leverages two external open source JavaScript resources. The first JavaScript library is called `stomp.js`, and was written by Jeff Mesnil. This library is included in the distribution for this book, but can also be found on GitHub: `https://github.com/jmesnil/stomp-websocket`. This library enables a JavaScript application to speak STOMP/WS with our WebSocket-enabled ActiveMQ message broker.

The second JavaScript library is jQuery, which we use for simplicity and helps us write our code in a more concise manner. We call our HTML and JavaScript files containing our application logic `index.html` and `rps.js`, respectively.

▓ **Note** We built our app jQuery version 1.8.2. The minified jQuery library, jquery-1.8.2.min, is included in the distribution of this book, but you can also download it from the official jQuery download site: http://jquery.com/download.

Building the HTML File

In this example, we keep our HTML code simple so that we can focus on the messaging logic of the application. After including the JavaScript libraries, we need to create the form fields and button for the players' names, as shown in Figure 5-11.

Figure 5-11. *Creating the form fields for the players' names*

Then, we create a div for the instructions and another one for the buttons, shown in Figure 5-12, which allows players to make their choice.

Figure 5-12. *Buttons representing the user's selection*

Finally, we have an empty div that will display the opponent's choice. Listing 5-6 shows the source code of our HTML file.

Listing 5-6. Source Code of the index.html File

```
<!DOCTYPE html>
<html>
<head>
    <title>Rock Paper Scissors - a WebSocket Demo</title>
    <!-- JavaScript libraries used: jQuery and the
        open source STOMP library -->
    <script src="js/jquery-1.8.2.min.js"></script>
    <script src='js/stomp.js'></script>
    <script src='js/rps.js'></script>
</head>
<body>
    <!-- Form fields and button for the players' names.
        The queues are named after the users -->
     <div id="nameFields">
     <input id="myName" type="text" placeholder="Your name"/>
```

```
<input id="opponentName" type="text" placeholder="Opponent's name"/>
<button id="goBtn" onclick="startGame();">
   Go
</button>
</div>
<!-- Instructions and buttons for the users to make their selections,
hidden initially -->
<div id="instructions" style="visibility:hidden;">
<p>Select one:</p>
</div>
<div id="buttons" style="visibility:hidden;">
<button id="rockBtn" name="rock" onclick="buttonClicked(this);">
   Rock
</button>
<button id="paperBtn" name="paper" onclick="buttonClicked(this);">
   Paper
</button>
<button id="scissorsBtn" name="scissors" onclick="buttonClicked(this);">
   Scissors
</button>
</div>
<!-- div to display opponent's choice, initially empty; populated by
JavaScript code in rps.js -->
<div id="opponentsButtons"></div>
</body>
</html>
```

Writing the Game Code

Now, that we've built a simple user interface for our app, let's take a closer look at the JavaScript code. First, we declare the variables, as shown in Listing 5-7. Notice that we include our connection URL to our WebSocket-enabled STOMP-based message broker, ActiveMQ.

Listing 5-7. Declaring the Variables Used in the JavaScript Code

```
// ActiveMQ STOMP connection URL
var url = "ws://0.0.0.0:61614/stomp";
// ActiveMQ username and password. Default value is "guest" for both.
var un, pw = "guest";

var client, src, dest;

// Variables holding the state whether the local and
// remote user had his/her turn yet
var hasUserPicked, hasOpponentPicked = false;
```

99

```
// HTML code for the opponent's three buttons and variable
// for opponent's pick
var opponentsBtns = '<button id="opponentRockBtn" name="opponentRock"
disabled="disabled">Rock</button>' + '<button id="opponentPaperBtn"
name="opponentPaper" disabled="disabled">Paper</button>' +
'<button id="opponentScissorsBtn" name="opponentScissors"
disabled="disabled">Scissors</button>';
var opponentsPick;

// Variables for this user's three buttons
var rockBtn, paperBtn, scissorsBtn;
```

After the DOM hierarchy has been fully constructed, we check whether the browser supports WebSocket. If it doesn't, we hide the divs that were rendered by the HTML page, and display a warning (Listing 5-8).

Listing 5-8. Checking Whether the Browser Supports WebSocket

```
// Testing whether the browser supports WebSocket.
// If it does, fields are rendered for users' names
$(document).ready(function() {
    if (!window.WebSocket) {
        var msg = "Your browser does not have WebSocket support. This
example will not work properly.";
        $("#nameFields").css("visibility", "hidden");
        $("#instructions").css("visibility", "visible");
        $("#instructions").html(msg);
    }
});
```

The startGame() function is invoked by the onclick event of the goBtn. This function, shown in Listing 5-9, disables all the elements of the previously filled out form, makes the instructions and button divs visible, and constructs the names for the source (src) and destination (dest) queues.

Listing 5-9. The startGame() Function

```
var startGame = function() {
    // Disabling the name input fields
    $("#myName").attr("disabled", "disabled");
    $("#opponentName").attr("disabled", "disabled");
    $("#goBtn").attr("disabled", "disabled");
    // Making the instructions and buttons visible
    $("#instructions").css("visibility", "visible");
    $("#buttons").css("visibility", "visible");
    // Queues are named after the players
```

```
    dest = "/queue/" + $("#opponentName").val();
    src = "/queue/" + $("#myName").val();
    connect();
};
```

The last function call of Listing 5-9 invokes the connect() function, which establishes the STOMP connection, displayed in Listing 5-10. The calls inside the connect() function are provided by the open source STOMP JavaScript library that we use: stomp.js.

Listing 5-10. The connect() Function, Establishing the STOMP Connection

```
// Establishing the connection
var connect = function() {
    client = Stomp.client(url);
    client.connect(un, pw, onconnect, onerror);
};
```

The client.connect API has two callback functions. The first, onconnect(), is invoked upon successful connection; the second, onerror(), is invoked when an error occurs.

Let's take a closer look at the onconnect() callback function. After a log to the console that we have successfully connected, we subscribe to the queue, defined by the src variable. This queue is named after this player. Whenever there's a message arriving in on this queue, the callback defined as the second parameter of client.subscribe will be executed. When the incoming message indicates that the opponent has already picked, we set the hasOpponentPicked to true. Then, we draw the buttons representing the opponent player's pick, but hide them if this player hasn't moved yet, shown in Listing 5-11.

Listing 5-11. Code Rendering the Game Buttons

```
// Function invoked when connection is established
var onconnect = function() {
    console.log("connected to " + url);
    client.subscribe(src, function(message) {
        console.log("message received: " + message.body);
        // The incoming message indicates that the
        // opponent had his/her turn (picked).
        // Therefore, we draw the buttons for the opponent.
        // If this user hasn't had his/her move yet,
        // we hide the div containing the buttons,
        // and only display them
        // when this user has had his/her move too.
        hasOpponentPicked = true;
        if (!hasUserPicked) {
            $("#opponentsButtons").css("visibility", "hidden");
```

```
            $("#instructions").html("<p>Your opponent is waiting for you.
Make your move!</p>");
        } else {
            $("#instructions").html("<p>Results:</p>");
            client.disconnect( function() {
                console.log("Disconnected...");
            });
        }
        $("#opponentsButtons").html(opponentsBtns);
        switch (message.body) {
            case "rock"     :
                opponentsPick = "#opponentRockBtn";
                break;
            case "paper"    :
                opponentsPick = "#opponentPaperBtn";
                break;
            case "scissors" :
                opponentsPick = "#opponentScissorsBtn";
                break;
        }
        $(opponentsPick).css("background-color", "yellow");
    });
    console.log("subscribed to " + src);
};
```

In case of an error, we can easily handle it using the onerror() callback function, shown in Listing 5-12. An easy way to test the execution of this function is by creating a connection first, and then stopping ActiveMQ. By doing so, you'll see an error message on the console indicating that the connection has been lost.

Listing 5-12. Capturing Errors with the onerror Callback Function

```
var onerror = function(error) {
    console.log(error);
};
```

The last function of our code is invoked when the user selects one of the three options: rock, paper, or scissors. The send() function of the client object takes three parameters: the destination, the headers (which is null in our case), and the message (the name of our button DOM object). We switch the hasUserPicked flag to true, indicating that the user has already picked. Then, we disable the form fields. Depending whether the opponent has moved, we either display the opponent's move, or change the instruction message, letting this player know that we're waiting for the opponent (Listing 5-13).

Listing 5-13. Adding Interaction to the User Selections (Rock, Paper, or Scissors)

```
// ActiveMQ STOMP connection URL
var url = "ws://0.0.0.0:61614/stomp";
// ActiveMQ username and password. Default value is "guest" for both.
var un, pw = "guest";

var client, src, dest;

// Variables holding the state whether the local and remote user had his/her
turn yet
var hasUserPicked, hasOpponentPicked = false;

// HTML code for the opponent's three buttons and
// variable for opponent's pick
var opponentsBtns = '<button id="opponentRockBtn" name="opponentRock"
disabled="disabled">Rock</button>' + '<button id="opponentPaperBtn"
name="opponentPaper" disabled="disabled">Paper</button>' +
'<button id="opponentScissorsBtn" name="opponentScissors"
disabled="disabled">Scissors</button>';
var opponentsPick;

// Variables for this user's three buttons
var rockBtn, paperBtn, scissorsBtn;

// Testing whether the browser supports WebSocket.
// If it does, fields are rendered for users' names
$(document).ready(function() {
    if (!window.WebSocket) {
        var msg = "Your browser does not have WebSocket support. This example
will not work properly.";
        $("#nameFields").css("visibility", "hidden");
        $("#instructions").css("visibility", "visible");
        $("#instructions").html(msg);
    }
});

// Getting started with the game. Invoked after
// this user's and opponent's name are submitted
var startGame = function() {
    // Disabling the name input fields
    $("#myName").attr("disabled", "disabled");
    $("#opponentName").attr("disabled", "disabled");
    $("#goBtn").attr("disabled", "disabled");
    // Making the instructions and buttons visible
    $("#instructions").css("visibility", "visible");
    $("#buttons").css("visibility", "visible");
    // Queues are named after the players
```

```javascript
    dest = "/queue/" + $("#opponentName").val();
    src = "/queue/" + $("#myName").val();
    connect();
};

// Establishing the connection
var connect = function() {
    client = Stomp.client(url);
    client.connect(un, pw, onconnect, onerror);
};

// Function invoked when connection is established
var onconnect = function() {
    console.log("connected to " + url);
    client.subscribe(src, function(message) {
        console.log("message received: " + message.body);
        // The incoming message indicates that the
        // opponent had his/her turn (picked).
        // Therefore, we draw the buttons for the opponent.
        // If this user hasn't had his/her move yet,
        // we hide the div containing the buttons, and only display
        // them when this user has had his/her move too.
        hasOpponentPicked = true;
        if (!hasUserPicked) {
            $("#opponentsButtons").css("visibility", "hidden");
            $("#instructions").html("<p>Your opponent is waiting for you. Make
your move!</p>");
        } else {
            $("#instructions").html("<p>Results:</p>");
            client.disconnect( function() {
                console.log("Disconnected...");
            });
        }
        $("#opponentsButtons").html(opponentsBtns);
        switch (message.body) {
            case "rock"     :
                opponentsPick = "#opponentRockBtn";
                break;
            case "paper"    :
                opponentsPick = "#opponentPaperBtn";
              break;
            case "scissors" :
                opponentsPick = "#opponentScissorsBtn";
                break;
        }
        $(opponentsPick).css("background-color", "yellow");
    });
```

```
      console.log("subscribed to " + src);
};

var onerror = function(error) {
      console.log(error);
};

var buttonClicked = function(btn) {
      client.send(dest, null, btn.name);
      hasUserPicked = true;
      console.log("message sent: " + btn.name);

      // Setting the background color of the button
      // representing the user's choice to orange.
      // Disabling all the buttons (to prevent changing the vote).
      $("#" + btn.id).css("background-color", "orange");
      $("#rockBtn").attr("disabled", "disabled");
      $("#paperBtn").attr("disabled", "disabled");
      $("#scissorsBtn").attr("disabled", "disabled");
      // Checking if the other user has moved yet. If so,
      // we display the buttons that were drawn beforehand
      // (see onconnect)
      if (hasOpponentPicked) {
         $("#opponentsButtons").css("visibility", "visible");
         $("#instructions").html("<p>Results:</p>");
         client.disconnect(function() {
            onerror = function() {};
            console.log("Disconnected...");
         });
      } else {
         $("#instructions").html("<p>Waiting for opponent...</p>");
      }
};
```

To run the app, ensure ActiveMQ is WebSocket-enabled (as shown in Listing 5-4), run ActiveMQ, and then open index.html in your WebSocket-enabled browser.

Monitoring Apache ActiveMQ

ActiveMQ provides a simple monitoring interface that gives you insight into what's happening under the covers. To access the management interface, click the Manage ActiveMQ broker link on the ActiveMQ Welcome page, or navigate to http://0.0.0.0:8161/admin/. After running the Rock Paper Scissors demo once, you will have two queues, one for each player. In our example, the opponents are Peter and Vanessa, and the queues are named after them. As Figure 5-13 shows, each queue has one consumer (the opponent player), and we sent one message to each queue (message enqueued). Both of these messages were dequeued soon thereafter (message dequeued).

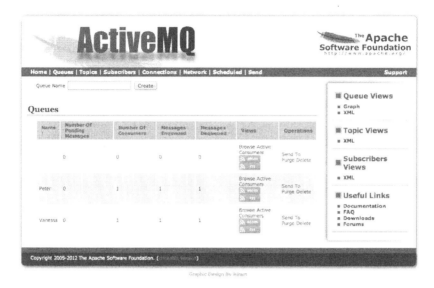

Figure 5-13. *The ActiveMQ management interface: monitoring message queues*

The management console also lists the currently active connections. In our demo, we have two active WebSocket connections, created through the ActiveMQ WebSocket Connector, shown in Figure 5-14.

Figure 5-14. *Active ActiveMQ connections created through the WebSocket Connector*

Suggested Extensions

While we've walked through building a very simple game to show messaging over WebSocket, there are many ways you can extend this game to make it more fully featured and even exciting. When playing rock-paper-scissors in person, finding out the winner is part of the excitement of the game. In an online environment, that's not quite the case. Declaring the winner would be a simple but significant enhancement to the app.

Another extension is to make the game more secure. Rather than relying on application logic to hide the opponent's move, you could centralize the game logic by creating a dedicated queue that accepts the moves, and another one that distributes the results. This logic would prevent players (or their browsers) from discovering the moves in advance. Additionally, you can use topics to inform all players about the game results, giving winning players publicity.

To improve player interaction, you could:

- Automatically match up lonely players who don't have opponents. A queue would be ideal for round-robin match making.

- Build a bot that uses artificial intelligence that players can choose as an opponent.

The Future of Web Messaging

Combining messaging concepts with low latency WebSocket communication opens the door to myriad incredible applications. As we have seen in this chapter, real-time collaborative "peer-to-peer" web and mobile applications can be built very easily. These applications can include shared document editing, interactive social presentation and learning tools, as well as social software with real time activity streams. Almost any type of audience can leverage such apps, including the consumer marketplace, education, health care, and transportation.

Another key application of web messaging is in the realm of machine-to-machine (M2M) communication. M2M, sometimes referred to as the "Internet of Things" (IoT), focuses on connecting everyday objects to the Internet. Implementing smart meters to track and automatically report utility usage, interacting with home appliances (such as checking if the door is locked or if the oven is turned off), installing credit-card-sized capable computers (such as the Raspberry Pi), monitoring devices and moving vehicles, telemetry, and augmented reality are just a few of the use cases that M2M addresses.

Most modern real-time enterprises employ a corporate services architecture as part of an efficient IT infrastructure. Diverse client facing or internal applications make requests to common services to efficiently deliver revenue and productivity. The notion of an Enterprise Service Bus (ESB) has been an accepted model for global corporations for more than ten years. WebSocket now allows these enterprise services to be extended securely to any web device allowing a more collaborative relationship with customers, partners, and mobile employees.

Complex Event Process engines can also benefit from WebSocket architectures by consuming, analyzing, and actively responding to events during the user's browser session, a mobile device, or a thick desktop client application.

In a similar fashion, BPMS (Business Process Management Systems) would be able to update the status of tasks that are part of large business processes executed throughout the enterprise and show to the user in real-time what's happening with relevant parts of the business.

The Web is clearly changing from a world of documents to a universe of activities where live applications, not documents, flourish. WebSocket is a key component of this new Web and will significantly transform how we use the Web in the enterprise and even in our daily lives. The nature of the WebSocket provides the same kind of connectivity that internal corporate clients already use to connect to the Enterprise Service Bus but extending them to the Web.

A new and evolving set of capabilities, grouped together under the Web RTC (Real Time Collaboration) umbrella with browser-based video and audio feeds are taking us beyond real-time data on an even more exhilarating journey.

Summary

In this chapter we reviewed the concepts of messaging, an architectural style characterized by sending asynchronous messages to build loosely coupled systems. You learned about the pub/sub pattern, as well as STOMP, an open messaging protocol. We explored an open-source STOMP and WebSocket-enabled message broker, Apache ActiveMQ. After learning about simple configuration changes, we ran the ActiveMQ STOMP-WebSocket demo, and then we built one on our own: rock-paper-scissors. Finally, we reviewed the monitoring and management capabilities of Apache ActiveMQ.

In the next chapter, we will use RFB, the protocol used by VNC, on top of WebSocket to build a real-time desktop sharing experience purely using HTML5.

CHAPTER 6

▨ ▨ ▨

VNC with the Remote Framebuffer Protocol

In the previous chapters, you learned how to layer two powerful protocols, XMPP and STOMP, over WebSocket. With these protocols, we were able to examine chat, presence, and messaging, all of which can be used to create rich applications and implement systems to power our browser-based world. In Chapter 4, we saw how we could use a widely used standard chat protocol with WebSocket and enabled a traditional desktop-based chat application to be used over the Web, as well as witnessed the benefits of layering WebSocket with a standard chat protocol. Similarly, in Chapter 5, we looked at how to interact with TCP-based message brokers from web applications. In both cases, we explored the transition between a traditional, desktop application-based world to a web-enabled world, and looked at how the full-duplex, low-latency connection over the Web provided by WebSocket can be beneficial to such applications. In this chapter, we look at an even more complex (yet standard) protocol and how to transform it using WebSocket as the communication platform.

With applications distributed among desktops using myriad operating systems, programs, and browser versions, it has become increasingly important for users to be system-agnostic, for Information Technology groups to be able to support any system from anywhere, and for application developers to be able to operate on any system. There are also times when users need to access a specific operating system. One popular way to access a specific system is using VNC (Virtual Network Computing).

VNC lets you share desktops over any network. It essentially allows you to view and control the interface of another computer remotely and can be thought of as the GUI (graphical user interface) equivalent to Telnet. You can also think of VNC as a long, virtual cable that enables you to view and control another desktop with its mouse, keyboard, and video signals.

As its name implies, VNC is used over networks. Due to challenges that we'll investigate in this chapter, VNC has not been easily used over the Web. With HTML5 and WebSocket, we can overcome some of these challenges and examine how highly portable rich Internet applications can leverage HTML5 and WebSocket to use VNC.

In this chapter, we'll explore how you can use WebSocket with the Remote Framebuffer (RFB) Protocol to expand virtual network computing to the Web. We'll also look at how, as a binary protocol, RFB uses the WebSocket API in a different way than the text-oriented protocols we discussed in the previous two chapters. After taking a look at RFB and VNC, we'll step through how to build a VNC client that connects to an open source VNC server using RFB over WebSocket. We'll walk through techniques used to enable screen sharing (a typical use case for VNC) over WebSocket and examine how to enable remote device input from a keyboard and mouse. Sound complex? RFB is indeed a more complex protocol than XMPP and STOMP.

The code examples that accompany this book contain the full, end-to-end RFB over WebSocket application that you can run against a VNC server. But, if you do not wish to work through the complexities of RFB, you can follow the steps in this chapter by referring to the Virtual Machine (VM) we provided (see Appendix B for instructions). The VM contains working code that you can run, examine, and digest at will. In the hands-on portion of this chapter, we'll highlight the code snippets in our application that are specifically pertinent to WebSocket and techniques for building an RFB over WebSocket client. After you explore the ideas in this chapter at a high level, you can run the code yourself and see how it all works together. Then, to analyze the code more closely, you can open the code examples in the VM.

The layering of RFB over WebSocket may not be for the fainthearted, but this compelling example contrasts to some of the more common WebSocket use cases like chat, as it illustrates the more interactive and graphical capabilities you can implement using HTML5 and WebSocket. Additionally, it shows how WebSocket can help bridge HTML5 and legacy systems.

■ **Note**   The VNC over WebSocket demo we use in this chapter was originally developed by Kaazing in 2010 to showcase WebSocket technology.

An Overview of Virtual Network Computing

The desktop metaphor for computing has been extremely popular for several decades. Historically, popular desktop operating systems have had networked windowing systems and remote access protocols that enabled the use of their systems from terminals and other PCs. Over the past few decades, the rise of the personal computer has also stimulated an explosion of desktop applications. Most of these desktop applications are now legacy applications, and not all of these legacy applications have comparable alternatives. VNC is a standard way to give users and systems the ability to continue to access legacy applications and systems, without concern for operating system compatibility. VNC also enables you to remotely interact with systems and applications on another computer as though you are actually using that computer.

Figure 6-1 shows a desktop controlling another computer's mouse and keyboard over the Web. The pixels of the remote display are duplicated on the controlling machine.

Figure 6-1. *Accessing the desktop of another PC over the Internet*

VNC is extremely useful for a multitude of purposes, from software testing and deployment to education. In a software development environment, you can test your application in a variety of combinations of operating systems, applications and application versions—all without leaving your own desktop. For example, you can test your new STOMP or XMPP over WebSocket application in any browser (legacy or not) on any type of system, such as Google Chrome on Mac OS. This ability can be extremely useful when you need to access legacy applications that are not available or that you cannot personally install.

VNC is also very useful for collaboration or education, where not only screen sharing is needed but also the ability to access another's desktop to assist with using a particular application. Imagine, for instance, an architecture student using a CAD (computer-aided design) application to design a room. A teaching assistant might be able to better explain to the student where to adjust dimensions without needing to have the CAD application installed on his or her own computer, and without needing to meet the student in person. Similarly, a technician can diagnose and fix a user's computer without needing to be on site.

There are several protocols for remotely accessing desktops. Some of these are platform specific, like Microsoft's Remote Desktop Protocol (RDP), X Window System or X11 (for UNIX, Linux, and Mac OS X), Chromoting (for the Google Chromebook), Apple Remote Desktop (ARD), and NX (for Linux and Solaris). Others, like Remote Framebuffer (RFB), are cross-platform.

VNC is an open source technology that is based on the RFB protocol and, as such, is platform independent. RFB is an IETF specification and is the basis for many VNC servers, as well as a thriving community that can help provide optimizations when you need them. Because it is so widely used, there are many resources available to help you get started and to help you get VNC working in your network.

While VNC is fairly ubiquitous and easy to implement in your network, VNC protocols have not typically worked well in web applications. There have been AJAX applications for remote desktop access, but they haven't been particularly optimal because HTTP's request-response communication is less than ideal for transmitting these protocols. Remote desktop applications are very bidirectional in nature. Users can perform input actions at any time. Likewise, the display can update at any time. A bidirectional transport layer protocol is critically important for making an efficient remote desktop application. There are plugin-based remote desktop applications that run in browsers, but with WebSocket we can bring these applications to pure HTML5 environments.

To better understand how the underlying technology for VNC works with WebSocket, let's take a closer look at RFB, as well as the difference between binary- and text-oriented protocols.

An Overview of the Remote Framebuffer Protocol

The Remote Framebuffer (RFB) protocol is an informational specification from the IETF (RFC 6143). While it is not an official standard, it is widely used and there are many interoperable implementations. RFC 6143 itself is over a decade old and has been revised several times.

Let's break down the protocol definition. A *framebuffer* is an array containing all of the pixel values displayed by a graphical computer system, and is the lowest common denominator model of a desktop computer. RFB is therefore a way to remotely access a framebuffer. For any system with a keyboard, mouse, and screen, there is probably a way to access it with RFB.

The RFB protocol was designed to have the server to do the "heavy lifting," enabling the client to be simple and thin. Clients built against the RFB protocol are also stateless, meaning that if the client disconnects and reconnects, the new session does not lose the state of the framebuffer.

Binary- and Text-Oriented Protocols

Protocols are generally oriented towards binary data or text strings. Binary protocols can be more compact than text-oriented protocols, and can neatly and naturally embed arbitrary binary data structures like images, audio and video. Binary protocols are intended to be read by machines rather than humans, and can optimize the data structure to be sent in any form to preserve efficiency.

Text-oriented protocols like STOMP and XMPP tend to transmit relatively larger messages on the wire and, as such, are more expensive to parse when compared with binary protocols. However, text-oriented protocols can be implemented by virtually any language, are readable by humans, and have flexible variable length fields. While binary protocols can be a more efficient way to transport data, text-oriented protocols may give you more flexibility, and can be easier to implement and deploy.

RFB is a binary protocol that transmits binary image data. The data can be compressed and can be streamed to and from servers with very high frequency updates. Image data can be streamed at high frequency from the server; similarly, clients can generate streams of input events caused by users moving their mice and pressing keys. These input events are compactly encoded in a binary format that takes very few bytes to transmit. The WebSocket Protocol can handle binary data or text strings. As such, binary WebSocket messages are a natural fit for the RFB protocol.

▓ **Note** Wireshark supports analyzing RFB protocol sessions, which can be useful when debugging a new implementation. For more information, see Chapter 3, where we discussed examining the WebSocket Protocol, and Appendix A, where we discuss dissecting and debugging WebSocket traffic using Wireshark.

Choosing to Use RFB over WebSocket

As we discussed in Chapter 4, you can build your own chat protocol; similarly, you could build your own remote access protocol that only works with your application. But, as we also mentioned, you would be missing out on the immense benefits of using a widely used, open, interoperable protocol. For example, there are numerous cross-platform servers designed for VNC available that are based on RFB, many of which are continually optimized and enhanced by a growing community of developers. As new operating systems are developed and versioned, you can work with the community to leverage the benefits, and focus on what you want your application to do.

In the next section, we walk through a basic example of using VNC, which illustrates how to use RFB over WebSocket: viewing another computer's screen using a web client and controlling it (with a keyboard and mouse). Figure 6-2 illustrates the flow of information in our example. Here, an RFB client runs in a browser tab and communicates with an RFB (VNC) server using a WebSocket to TCP proxy between the web client and RFB server. Using this client, a user can view and control a remote desktop entirely within a web application over WebSocket and RFB.

Figure 6-2. Connecting with RFB over WebSocket

Building a VNC (RFB) Client over WebSocket

Now that we've examined some of the concepts behind VNC over WebSocket, let's take a look at a working example.

⫶ **Note**   For the purposes of this section, while "VNC" refers to remote desktop connections that use RFB as the underlying protocol, we will refer to the components that use RFB for VNC as "RFB components" (specifically, the "RFB client" and "RFB server"). By using RFB, you effectively build a VNC application.

In this example, we look at how we can combine this popular and widely used technology with WebSocket. We examine the key components of an RFB client we built using HTML5 and WebSocket, which can view and control the graphical user interface of another computer.

We've seen how WebSocket can elevate HTML5 applications to first class network participants. The client application in this section is much like a desktop RFB client in every way, except it is implemented using web technology and runs in the browser. We also add remote device input, which allows you to control the other GUI with your keyboard and mouse. The steps in this section not only show you how to control the GUI of a remote computer over RFB and WebSocket, you might find this example inspirational when building your own graphical applications that use WebSocket. Finally, we examine some of the exciting applications that you can build that will let your users remotely control another computer—all from within a browser tab.

The client side of this application is split into two layers. The protocol library, RfbClient.js, comprises an implementation of the RFB protocol in JavaScript. This library handles the RFB syntax defined by the specification that is understood by all compatible servers.

The user interface of the client is composed of vnc.html, ui.js, and vnc.css. These files define the page structure, application behavior, and appearance of the VNC application, respectively. On the server side, we use a Node.js script to proxy WebSocket connections to TCP connections. This proxy connects to a backend RFB server running on a remote desktop.

Setting Up a Proxy Server

RFB is an application layer protocol that uses TCP for its transport layer. This layering should be fairly familiar by now, as it is a common theme shared by the protocols in the previous two chapters. As discussed in Chapter 4, when using a standard TCP protocol over WebSocket, you have a choice between upgrading the server to accept WebSocket connections and using a proxy to relay between WebSocket and TCP.

In the example shown in Listing 6-1, we use a simple proxy adapted from the Node.js server we wrote in Chapter 3. This proxy is unaware of RFB and is completely application agnostic. It simply handles incoming WebSocket connections and makes outgoing TCP connections. Data streams in as WebSocket messages on one side of the proxy and out as TCP on the other. In our completed application, the proxy will handle connections from our RFB client and proxy the WebSocket connection over TCP to the back-end RFB server. Refer to Figure 6-2 in the previous section, which shows where the proxy server lies in our architecture.

Listing 6-1. Proxy Server Code

```
var websocket = require("./websocket-example");
var net = require("net");

var remotePort = 5900;
var remoteHost = "192.168.56.101";

websocket.listen(8080, "localhost", function(websocket) {
    // set up backend TCP connection
    var tcpsocket = new net.Socket({type:"tcp4"});
    tcpsocket.connect(remotePort, remoteHost);

    // TCP handler functions
    tcpsocket.on("connect", function() {
      console.log("TCP connection open");
    });
    tcpsocket.on("data", function(data) {
      websocket.send(data);
    });
    tcpsocket.on("error", function() {
      console.log("TCP connection error", arguments);
    });
```

```
    // WebSocket handler functions
    websocket.on("data", function(opcode, data) {
        tcpsocket.write(data);
    });
    websocket.on("close", function(code, reason) {
        console.log("WebSocket closed")
        // close backend connection
        tcpsocket.end();
    });

    console.log("WebSocket connection open");
});
```

While there are many RFB servers that accept WebSocket connections directly, you have the flexibility to use any compatible RFB server with this example. Note, though, that because the binding of RFB onto WebSocket has not been specified, there may be some potential complications and incompatibility. In our example, we use the popular and widely used open source TightVNC server (which is based on RFB) on a virtual machine. TightVNC does not currently support WebSocket natively, but works with our proxy server.

The address of the virtual machine is hard coded into the proxy script. Hardcoding the address is convenient for development but is *not* suitable for production. To use this in your environment, you may need to change the hostname and port variables. Also, we should emphasize that neither the WebSocket server nor the VNC server in this example authenticates incoming connections, which is extremely unwise for any purpose other than a simple demonstration. See Chapter 7 for better security practices.

The RFB Client

Now that we have set up a proxy server that can accept RFB over WebSocket connections, we can build the front-end portion, or the client. While the RFB client is thin in nature, we want it to be able to view the screen of the RFB server, which involves receiving graphical information about what is happening on that screen. We also want to be able to control the remote computer (also known as the RFB server).

In this section, we explore:

- Building a simple client in JavaScript
- Techniques for working with the binary data from the RFB protocol and the WebSocket Protocol
- Connecting to the server
- Enabling the client to accept framebuffer updates
- Using HTML5 <canvas> to render a framebuffer
- Handling device input

Implementing RFB in JavaScript

The client side of this RFB application is an HTML5 application that runs in the browser. It makes use of HTML, CSS, and JavaScript. The basic user interface is defined by some HTML markup. The logic of the application, including a library to communicate using the RFB protocol, is written in JavaScript.

Listing 6-2 shows the starting HTML that includes the protocol library and application scripts:

Listing 6-2. Starting HTML with Protocol Library and Application Scripts

```
<!DOCTYPE html>
<title>RFB over WebSocket</title>

<script src="bytes.js"></script>
<script src="RfbClient.js"></script>
<script src="ui.js"></script>
```

■ **Pro Tip**   Because JavaScript is purely event-driven, there is no way to wait inside of a running function for more bytes to become available. Every function must run to completion and return quickly. To enable a JavaScript application to receive RFB protocol messages, we map the protocol to event handlers that can run in the browser. This design technique is useful for implementing many different types of protocols.

Working with Byte Streams

In Chapter 2, we demonstrated how to send and receive binary data with the WebSocket API. Writing binary messages is as simple as calling WebSocket.send() with Blob and ArrayBuffer arguments. Reading binary messages is automatic, as the type of incoming message events matches WebSocket.binaryType. It is straightforward to communicate using WebSocket messages using the WebSocket API, and to implement protocols with a message-aligned binding to the WebSocket Protocol. In contrast, arbitrary application-level protocols like RFB are not aligned to WebSocket frames. The syntax of such a protocol is defined in terms of streams of bytes. Each call to WebSocket.onmessage is not guaranteed to contain one and only one complete RFB message. RFB messages can be fragmented or conflated into more or fewer than the expected number of WebSocket messages. A stream abstraction can be useful to bridge the gap between the two modes of communication.

In Listing 6-3, the file bytes.js contains utilities used by RfbClient.js to simplify reading and writing byte streams. In particular, it contains a CompositeStream API that joins sequences of discrete ArrayBuffers into logical streams of bytes. When binary WebSocket messages arrive, RfbClient.js calls CompositeStream.append() to add the new bytes to the inbound stream. To read and parse messages at the RFB protocol level, RFB handler code calls CompositeStream.consume() to pull bytes out of the stream. Similarly, RfbClient.js uses functions in bytes.js to write numbers as bytes in messages to the server. These functions make use of the standard DataView type, calling setter methods on the ArrayBuffers with bytes representing 8, 16, and 32 bit integers. Listing 6-3 shows the numerical functions in bytes.js.

Listing 6-3. Numerical functions in bytes.js

```
$prototype.appendBytes = function appendBytes() {
    ba = new Uint8Array(arguments);
    this.append(ba.buffer);
}

$prototype.appendUint16 = function appendUint16(n) {
    var b = new ArrayBuffer(2);
    var dv = new DataView(b);
    dv.setUint16(0, n);
    this.append(b);
}

$prototype.appendUint32 = function appendUint32(n) {
    var b = new ArrayBuffer(4);
    var dv = new DataView(b);
    dv.setUint32(0, n);
    this.append(b);
}
```

These functions make it easier to write arrays of bytes containing messages in the syntax of the RFB protocol.

Setting Up the Connection

The RfbProtocolClient connect function sets the initial client state and creates an empty stream, a WebSocket, and event handlers for that socket. This function also sets the first readHandler to versionHandler, since the RFB protocol starts with an exchange of version information between the server and client. Listing 6-4 shows the RfbProtocolClient connect function we must set up to connect to our server. The connect function also constructs an empty CompositeStream. That stream will contain bytes representing partial RFB messages from the server.

Listing 6-4. RfbProtocolClient Connect Function

```
RfbProtocolClient = function() {};

$prototype = RfbProtocolClient.prototype;

$prototype.connect = function(url) {
    this.socket = new WebSocket(url);
    this.socket.binaryType = "arraybuffer";
    this.stream = new CompositeStream();

    bindSocketHandlers(this, this.socket);
```

```
    this.buttonMask = 0;
    // set first handler
    this.readHandler = versionHandler;
}
```

The bindSocketHandlers() function sets up the WebSocket event handlers used by this protocol client. The message handler does something interesting: it adds any incoming data to the byte stream and calls the current read handler, then continues calling the current read handler until that handler returns false. This function allows the message handler to effectively loop over the incoming data and process any number of messages. If there is a partial message left in the stream, it remains there until the socket produces another message event. At that time, the read handler that last returned false is called again. The presence of additional bytes might cause that handler to then return true. Listing 6-5 shows the bindSocketHandlers() function.

Listing 6-5. The bindSocketHandlers() Function

```
var bindSocketHandlers = function($this, socket) {
    socket.onopen = function(e) {
        // Ignore WebSocket open event.
        // The server will send the first message.
    }

    var stream = $this.stream;
    socket.onmessage = function messageHandler(e) {
        // Append bytes to stream.
        stream.append(e.data);
        // Read handler loop.
        while($this.readHandler($this, stream)) {
            // Do nothing.
        }
    }

    socket.onclose = socket.onerror = function() {
        console.log("Connection closed", arguments);
    }
}
```

Each event handler expects a certain number of bytes to be able to read a complete message. If there are fewer bytes in the incoming stream, the handler returns false, which puts the WebSocket message event handler back into a waiting state. If there are enough bytes to read a complete protocol data message, the handler reads that many bytes out of the stream, processes them, and returns true. Each handler can also set the next handler variable before returning true.

In Listing 6-6, the versionHandler() function sets the readHandler variable to numSecurityTypesHandler, because the next state the client enters reads a message containing the number of security types supported by the server.

Listing 6-6. The versionHandler() Function

```
var versionHandler = function($this, stream) {
    if (stream.length < 12) {
        return false;
    }

    var version = new Uint8Array(stream.consume(12));
    // Echo back version.
    sendBytes($this, version.buffer)

    // Set next handler.
    $this.readHandler = numSecurityTypesHandler;
    return true;
}
```

Enabling the Client to Accept Framebuffer Updates

Once you've connected the client to the server, the client must send a message requesting framebuffer updates. Doing so will enable the client to receive the data from the RFB server.

The RFB protocol defines different types of framebuffer updates. Each type is indicated with a numerical code in the protocol message. In this example, we will only use two basic encoding types: Raw and CopyRect. Raw, as you might guess, represents pixel data as a raw, uncompressed bitmap. CopyRect is an instruction from the server to copy a portion of the current bitmap elsewhere on the screen. Since many user interfaces contain large solid color regions, this can be a very efficient way to update a client screen.

When no more rectangles remain in the stream, the client can request another update. This implementation, as shown in Listing 6-7, is a compromise between polling for and streaming the data in order to throttle server-sent updates without being too chatty.

Listing 6-7. Framebuffer Requests

```
var doUpdateRequest = function doUpdateRequest($this, incremental) {
    var request = new CompositeStream();

    request.appendBytes(3);              // type (u8 3)
    request.appendBytes(1);              // incremental

    request.appendBytes(0,0,0,0);        // top left corner: x (u16 0) y (u16 0)
    request.appendUint16($this.width);   // width (u16 800)
    request.appendUint16($this.height);  // height (u16 600)

    sendBytes($this, request.consume(request.length));
}
```

Listing 6-7 shows the framebuffer requests, which specify the position of the top left corner of the area to update. They also contain the height and width of the region, which allows clients to elect to update only a portion of the framebuffer. For this example, we will always request updates across the entire canvas. The incremental byte indicates to the server that the client has a copy of the current framebuffer and can apply updates. That is more efficient than sending the entire contents of the screen over and over again.

Using HTML5 <canvas> to Draw a Framebuffer

Now that the client can accept framebuffer updates, let's render this information on the client, which enables the client to view the GUI information coming from the RFB server (or TightVNC in our case).

One of the most important new elements in HTML5 is <canvas>. The <canvas> element supports a 2d drawing API that gives HTML5 applications the ability to manipulate pixel graphics. Low-level drawing is required to efficiently display a framebuffer in an application, because application code must be able to set each pixel color individually.

Listing 6-8 creates a canvas element, sets its initial width and height, and gets a drawing context.

Listing 6-8. Creating a Canvas Element

```
Screen = function(width, height) {
    this.canvas = document.createElement("canvas");
    this.canvas.setAttribute("height", height);
    this.canvas.setAttribute("width", width);
    this.context = this.canvas.getContext("2d");
}
```

The 2d drawing context provides the drawing API for interacting with the canvas element. Many of the 2d context functions deal with drawing primitive shapes. Functions such as fillRect are ideal for displaying most programmatically generated graphics. To display a framebuffer, we need to use the lower level functions exposed by the canvas 2d context. The putImageData() function is an ideal low-level pixel function, directly setting the pixel values of a canvas from an array of color data. Listing 6-9 shows an example of this function.

Listing 6-9. The putImageData() Function

```
context.putImageData(imageData, xPos, yPos);
```

Similarly, there is a getImageData() function that can retrieve pixel values from a canvas context, as shown in Listing 6-10.

Listing 6-10. The a getImageData() Function

```
context.getImageData(xSrc, ySrc, width, height);
```

We will use these canvas functions to update the canvas with framebuffer updates from the RFB protocol. Conveniently, ImageData is a type that is compatible with the binary messages sent and received by WebSocket. In fact, in modern browsers, getImageData() returns a Uint8ClampedArray, one of the TypedArray views that can wrap array buffers.

▓ **Note** Older browsers with canvas support use an obsolete ImageData type, which is not a typed array; it must be converted into one.

To render the client framebuffer, RfbClient.js handles two kinds of updates: Raw and CopyRect. More advanced clients can also handle other pixel encodings.

Raw Pixel Data

The simplest framebuffer update consists of raw pixel data. Raw pixels are indicated with encoding type zero (0x0) in the RFB protocol. Listing 6-11 shows the pixel data, which consists simply of red, green, and blue values for every pixel in the updated portion of the framebuffer.

Listing 6-11. Raw Pixel Data

```
$prototype.putPixels = function putPixels(array, width, height, xPos, yPos) {
    var imageData = this.context.createImageData(width, height);
    copyAndTransformImageData(array, imageData);
    this.context.putImageData(imageData, xPos, yPos);
}
```

CopyRect

The second encoding type used in this example is copyRect, which is encoding type one (0x01) in the RFB protocol. This function is a clever operation that is well suited to conveying framebuffer updates that mostly consist of the same repeated pixel values.

Just like the raw encoding, copyRect rectangle messages specify position, width, and height. This information represents the target rectangle in the framebuffer that will be filled by the update. Instead of also sending the current pixel data for that rectangle, however, copyRect messages have just two more payload values: the X and Y position of a source rectangle. The source rectangle has the same width and height as the destination or target rectangle. Every pixel from the source is copied verbatim into the corresponding pixel in the destination area.

To implement copyRect, we need both getImageData and putImageData. The copyRect() function contains the location, width, and height of the source pixels along with the location of the destination pixels. It operates on the framebuffer canvas in much the same was as the raw putPixels function does, except it takes its pixel data from the current canvas. Listing 6-12 shows the copyRect() function with getImageData and putImageData.

Listing 6-12. The copyRect() Function

```
$prototype.copyRect = function copyRect(width, height, xPos, yPos, xSrc, ySrc){
  // get pixel data from the current framebuffer
  var imageData = this.context.getImageData(xSrc, ySrc, width, height);
  // put pixel data in target region
  this.context.putImageData(imageData, xPos, yPos);
```

Other Encodings and Efficiency

While sending raw pixels over the Internet is very inefficient, copyRect is extremely efficient when you are lucky enough to have repeated pixel values in your framebuffer. Real desktops are more complex than this, so there are more advanced encodings that can be used to reduce bandwidth usage of RFB. These encodings use compression algorithms to reduce the bandwidth required to send pixel data. For example, encoding 16 (0x10) uses ZLIB for compression. This is the style of encoding you would ideally like to use in a real RFB-based application. Most RFB clients and servers support compressed updates.

Handling Input in the Client

So far we've built enough of an RFB client to be able to observe a desktop updating in real time (in effect, screen sharing). In order to interact with that desktop, we need to handle user input, which will allow the RFB client to control the mouse and keyboard of the RFB server. In this section, we examine how to accept the mouse and keyboard input on the client and communicate that input information to the RFB server.

Client to Server Messages

The RFB protocol defines types of messages that the client sends to the server. These message types indicate what kind of message the client sends to the server. As previously described, the message type is the first byte of the client to server message and is represented by an integer. Table 6-1 describes what kinds of message types exist in the RFB specification.

Table 6-1. Message Types in the RFB Specification

Message Type Number	Message Type
0	SetPixelFormat
2	SetEncodings
3	FramebufferUpdateRequest
4	KeyEvent
5	PointerEvent
6	ClientCutText

In this section, we will focus on RFB client to server message types 4 and 5, keyboard and mouse events respectively.

Mouse Input

Handling mouse and keyboard input is an important part of our sample implementation and represents the capturing actions from the keyboard and mouse clicks. These actions trigger JavaScript events that are sent from the client to the server. This lets VNC users control applications running on remote systems. In our application, we will detect input events in JavaScript and send the corresponding RFB protocol messages over our open WebSocket.

In the RFB protocol, a PointerEvent represents either movement or a pointing device button press or release. The PointerEvent message is a binary event message consisting of a message-type byte that specifies what kind of message is being sent to the server (for example, a pointing device click, a pointing device movement, and so on), a button-mask byte which carries the current state of the pointing device buttons from 1 to 8 that are represented by the bits 0 to 7 where 0 means the button is up and 1 means the button is down or pressed, and two position values each consisting of an unsigned short integer that represents the X and Y coordinates in relation to the screen (see Figure 6-3).

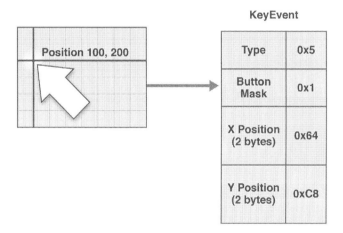

Figure 6-3. *Pressing the left mouse button generates a binary PointerEvent message of 6 bytes*

Listing 6-13 shows the mouse event.

Listing 6-13. Mouse Event

```
var doMouseEvent = function ($this, e) {
    var event = new CompositeStream();

    event.appendBytes(5);      // type (u8 5)
    event.appendBytes($this.buttonMask);
```

```
    // position
    event.appendUint16(e.offsetX);
    event.appendUint16(e.offsetY);

    sendBytes($this, event.consume(event.length));
}
```

Listing 6-14 indicates that when mouse motion is detected, a mouse event is sent to the VNC server.

Listing 6-14. Mouse Event to the VNC Server

```
$prototype.mouseMoveHandler = function($this, e) {
 doMouseEvent($this, e);
}
```

Similarly, when a mouse click is detected, the button that was clicked is transmitted as a mouse event, as shown in Listing 6-15.

Listing 6-15. Transmitting a Mouse Click as a Mouse Event

```
$prototype.mouseDownHandler = function($this, e) {
    if (e.which == 1) {
        // left click
        $this.buttonMask ^= 1;
    } else if (e.which == 3) {
        // right click
        $this.buttonMask ^= (1<<2);
    }
    doMouseEvent($this, e);
}
```

Table 6-2 describes the mouse event types that are relevant to the RFB event listeners.

Table 6-2. *Mouse Event Types*

Event Type	Description
mousedown	Indicates that the pointing device was pressed down over an element
mouseup	Indicates that the pointing device was released over an element
mouseover	Indicates that the pointing device is over an element
mousemove	Indicates that the pointing device is moved while it is over an element

Keyboard Input

In addition to the PointerEvent messages, the RFB protocol specifies that KeyEvent messages indicate a key was pressed or released. The KeyEvent message is a binary event message consisting of a message-type byte which specifies what kind of message is being sent to the server (a keyboard event in this case), a down-flag byte that indicates if the key is pressed when the value is 1 or if the key is now released if the value is 0, two bytes of padding and the key itself specified in the four bytes of the key field. Figure 6-4 shows the relationship between the keyboard input and the KeyEvent.

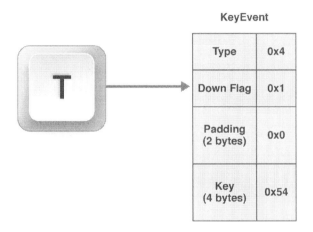

Figure 6-4. *Pressing the 'T' key generates a binary KeyEvent message of 8 bytes*

The RFB protocol uses the same key codes as the X Window System even if the client (or server) is not running the X Window System. These codes are not the same as the key codes on DOM KeyboardEvents, so a mapping function is necessary. Listing 6-16 shows the KeyEvent function for our example.

Listing 6-16. The KeyEvent() Function

```
var doKeyEvent = function doKeyEvent($this, key, downFlag) {
    var event = new CompositeStream();

    event.appendBytes(4);      // type (u8 4)
    event.appendBytes(downFlag);
    event.appendBytes(0,0);    // padding

    event.appendUint32(key);

    sendBytes($this, event.consume(event.length));
}
```

In Listing 6-16, the doKeyEvent() function takes a key value and a downFlag and constructs the corresponding RFB client message. The padding bytes seem wasteful. They clearly are today, since network bandwidth and latency are more precious than CPU cycles. Aligning integer values to 32-bit boundaries is a vestigial optimization in the protocol design that trades bytes of network bandwidth for processing speed on some computing platforms. Since we are generating these values in JavaScript, which doesn't even have a 32-bit integer type, it looks pretty funny!

■ **Note**　Keyboard events are device-dependent, which means a mapping with the operating system must occur for the keyboard events to be generated.

Table 6-3 describes the DOM Keyboard Event Types.

Table 6-3. *DOM Keyboard Event Types*

Event Type	Description
keydown	Indicates that a specific key was pressed on the keyboard and triggers before the keypress event
keyup	Indicates that a specific key was released

This example uses the event.which property to detect keyboard keys. The property is a legacy DOM API, but is suitable for the purposes of this example. The event.which property returns the value of the character represented by the key that was pressed or released. We can map that value to the key value used by RFB in KeyEvent messages.

Putting It All Together

At this point, we are ready to connect to a RFB server and start using a remote desktop. Open vnc.html in a modern browser that supports the required JavaScript APIs. This will probably work from your local file system. Otherwise, serve all of the static files for this example from a location where you can reach them with your browser.

Start the WebSocket-to-TCP proxy and the back-end RFB server. When you press the Connect button in your application, you should see a remote desktop appear in your browser tab. Try using the UI of the remote system. It's magical.

■ **Note**　Keep in mind that you can simply install and launch the server and client from the VM. See Appendix B for more information.

Enhancing the Application

To enhance this application, you have a few obvious options. For one, you can try removing the WebSocket to TCP proxy and connect directly to an RFB server that contains integrated WebSocket support. You can also implement other RFB features; RFB supports many other pixel encoding mechanisms not included in this example. There are negotiable authentication mechanisms, as well, that you can add support for. Furthermore, RFB servers can be configured to support different color depths. You could add these modes to the RFB client protocol library.

With the power of VNC/RFB over WebSocket technology you should be able to design a web application that connects to multiple desktops on the same web page as a way to work with them. Imagine that you have three panels on a web page and each one of them is connected to a remote system through VNC over WebSocket where you can perform an action on one that is controlling a Windows system, switch to another panel that controls a Linux system, then finally focus on the third panel that controls a Mac OS. While these three remote systems are running for you in parallel, you can perform additional tasks in your browser or on your desktop.

The mechanism you learned in this chapter is only the beginning of what you could develop with WebSocket in terms of simultaneously connecting remotely to several different machines from a single web page without installing anything on your system.

Summary

In this chapter, we discussed some key points from the history of network computing, specifically virtual network computing. We examined the widely implemented Remote Framebuffer (RFB) protocol, stepped through how to layer RFB and WebSocket to enable you to control the GUI of another computer remotely, and highlighted key techniques for using RFB with WebSocket. We also looked at some of the educational and technical benefits of VNC over WebSocket, as well as a comparison of binary-oriented and text-oriented protocols. We also explored potentially exciting uses and applications you can build to enable users to perform tasks they couldn't before, like viewing and controlling multiple desktops from the same web page.

Now that we've stepped through a few real-life demos and use cases of WebSocket, we'll discuss WebSocket security and how to secure WebSocket applications in the next chapter.

CHAPTER 7

■ ■ ■

WebSocket Security

The chapters in this book so far have shown you how WebSocket enables full-duplex, bidirectional communication over the Web. We've looked at how layering WebSocket with commonly used standard protocols like XMPP and STOMP enables you to take your TCP-based architectures to the Web and allow your applications to be accessed from almost anywhere. You also learned how you can enable remote control of systems over the Internet using VNC.

With these abilities comes the challenge and complexity of security. Web security is a topic that is as important as it is misunderstood. Although aspects of a software system can be designed with security in mind, the properties of a system that are relevant to security can be very complex due to the interactions of many different components. Enhancing security on the system means applying techniques to the software system to protect against threats.

The topic of Web security spans network and browser security, including application-level security and even the security of operating systems. When you enable your users to access systems over the Internet, you expose your assets (your database, server, application, and so on) to all types of intended and unintended risks. Web security techniques mitigate and address threats over the Internet.

The WebSocket standard handles core security by providing for unencrypted and encrypted transport, and by defining WebSocket as a frame within which all existing security protocols can operate. We cannot prove that WebSocket itself possesses something called "security" or offer any final, bulletproof recipes. We can, however, examine specific types of threats related to WebSocket and recommend best practices to help write and deploy more secure applications.

This chapter describes WebSocket security in detail, explains security decisions made in the protocol and API designs, and recommends practices for deploying WebSocket services and applications. There are numerous Web security resources available that you should read, particularly those relating to any protocols you want to layer with WebSocket. In this chapter, we focus on aspects of security that pertain directly to WebSocket.

WebSocket Security Overview

Deploying applications over the Web presents security challenges you must consider when deciding to use WebSocket. Such challenges include attacks on servers that may exploit flaws in WebSocket servers in order to gain control over them. There are also

129

denial of service attacks, which are attempts to make resources unavailable for the system's users. The goal of such attacks is to prevent a web site, service, or server from working efficiently—temporarily or even indefinitely.

Allowing users to access your web applications can also expose your users to attacks. Malicious persons and evil robots are constantly attempting to copy, delete, and modify precious user data. Some of these attacks may rely on impersonation, while others may be more passive eavesdropping and interception. These common threats are typically mitigated using authentication and encrypted communication.

In addition to these well-known types of attacks, there are unintended and ambiguous attacks against those who are neither using nor deploying WebSocket. Examples of these include legacy proxy and monitoring systems that confuse WebSocket traffic and HTTP traffic.

Many of the WebSocket Protocol design choices that we examined in Chapter 3 make sense in light of security and were added to mitigate specific attacks. After all, if the purpose of WebSocket is to open a free-flowing pipe of bytes between two endpoints, then everything else is decorative. As it happens, some of these trappings are necessary to thwart very specific types of attacks. These threats may affect users of the protocol, or more curiously, innocent bystanders who happen to be on the same network.

Table 7-1 describes some of these security issues and a brief description of how some features of the WebSocket Protocol were specifically designed to mitigate these attacks. We'll delve more into each of these areas in the subsequent sections, and explore higher-level WebSocket security areas like authentication and application-level security.

Table 7-1. *Types of Attacks Addressed by the WebSocket API and Protocol*

This Type of Attack	. . . is Addressed by this WebSocket API or Protocol Feature
Denial of service	Origin header
Denial of service by connection flooding	Throttling new connections using the Origin header
Proxy server attacks	Masking
Man-in-the middle, eavesdropping	WebSocket Secure (`wss://`)

WebSocket Security Features

Before we examine the aspects of the WebSocket API and Protocol that address specific areas of security, let's review the WebSocket handshake. The WebSocket handshake contains several of the components that help establish security on the WebSocket connection.

As we described in Chapter 3, WebSocket connections begin with an HTTP request containing special headers. The contents of that request were very carefully designed for security and compatibility with HTTP. To review, Listing 7-1 is an example of a client sending WebSocket handshake:

Listing 7-1. Client Initiating a WebSocket Handshake

```
Request
GET /echo HTTP/1.1
Host: echo.websocket.org
Origin: http://www.websocket.org
Sec-WebSocket-Key: 7+C6O0xYybOv2zmJ69RQsw==
Sec-WebSocket-Version: 13
Upgrade: websocket
```

The server sends back a response, as shown in Listing 7-2.

Listing 7-2. Server Responding to and Completing a WebSocket Handshake

```
Response
101 Switching Protocols
Connection: Upgrade
Date: Wed, 20 Jun 2012 03:39:49 GMT
Sec-WebSocket-Accept: fYoqiH14DgI+5ylEMwM2sOLzOiO=
Server: Kaazing Gateway
Upgrade: WebSocket
```

Two significant areas in the handshake to note are the `Origin` header and the `Sec-` headers, which we'll examine in the next sections.

Origin Header

The WebSocket Protocol (RFC 6455) was published at the same time as another document that defines a key idea necessary for WebSockets to be safely deployed across the Web: origin. The origin concept appears in earlier specifications such as Cross-Document Messaging and Cross-Domain Resource Sharing, and is widely used today. However, in order for the WebSocket standard to be usefully and safely rolled out to the Web, the origin concept needed to be more precisely defined. RFC 6454 achieves this by defining and describing the principles behind the same origin policy and, more importantly, the origin header.

▓ **Note** For the complete RFC 6454 specification, see
`http://www.ietf.org/rfc/rfc6454.txt`.

Origins consist of a scheme, host, and port. In serialized form, an origin looks like a URL: the scheme and host are separated by `://` and a colon precedes the port. For origins where the port matches the default port for the scheme, the port is omitted.

> ░ **Note** Since most serialized origins use port 80, which matches the default HTTP port, the port is commonly omitted from the origin. A typical serialized origin looks like this:
> `http://example.com`

Figure 7-1 shows an example origin, containing a scheme, host, and port.

Figure 7-1. *Diagram of an origin*

If any component of two origins differs, browsers treat those origins as completely separate origins. Browsers can enforce consistent rules for communicating and sharing data between origins. For instance, applications with different origins can communicate using the `postMessage()` API, but they are able to scope their messages based on the origins of the sender and receiver.

Origin replaces older, less standardized, and more complex rules, sometimes referred to as the "same-domain policy." The same-domain policy was not comprehensive: pages could still hotlink images and embed iframes from any origin. This policy included rules for the `referer` header, which in addition to being spelled incorrectly by the specification, included URL paths and thereby leaked too much information. As a result, referers were frequently hidden and could not be relied on for access control. For cross-domain scripting, non-standard rules were enforced for pages with partially matching origins that differed only by port or scheme. In short, the same-domain policy was a mess.

The origin model cleans up all the cross-domain rules for web applications. It defines an origin as the trio (scheme, host, and port). If two URLs differ at all in one of those three ways, they have different origins.

The origin model also makes it possible to host public and semi-public services. For example, a server could allow several origins, allowing connections to exchange data with applications all over the Web. A public service could even try allowing every origin by default, blocking only those origins known to be problematic. As such, origin is more flexible than older same-domain policies under which *all* non-similar origins were assumed to be malicious and were blocked by default.

Mitigating Denial of Service

Origin allows the receiving party to reject connections that it does not want to handle. Web servers can inspect the origin header of incoming requests and choose not to handle connections from unknown or possibly malicious origins. This ability can be extremely helpful in mitigating denial of service (DoS) attacks.

Denial of service attacks against web servers come in many flavors. Some DoS attacks begin from botnets consisting of thousands of compromised PCs; such attacks are completely under the control of the attacker. Some may consider that botnets are just a part of modern life on the Internet. There are other attacks, however, that web origin security can address directly. The web platform can make it more challenging to abuse features of the Web to launch DoS attacks. In the case of WebSocket, because receiving servers can use the origin header to verify the origin of incoming requests, DoS attacks are much more difficult to accomplish. Servers can ban connections from unknown or attacking origins, saving server resources by rejecting connections.

The proper origin header is included in all WebSocket requests made by browsers. What about applications that don't run in browsers at all? You may notice that there is nothing stopping you from opening a socket in a console application and writing any origin you like. Servers don't really know that a request with a particular origin header came from a web application; all they know is that a request did *not* come from a web application from a different origin. One question people ask over and over again is, if origin is so easily spoofed, what security does it provide? Understanding the answer requires understanding the true nature of WebSockets, as described in the next section.

What is a WebSocket (from a Security Perspective)?

If you've made it this far in this book, you know the many benefits afforded by using WebSocket in your applications. As described in Chapter 1, WebSocket has many desirable features. WebSocket is a simple, standard, full-duplex protocol with low overhead that can be used to build scalable, near real-time network servers. If you're an astute student of computing or recall slightly earlier days, you know that most of these traits apply equally well to plain, unadulterated TCP/IP. That is, they are traits of sockets (in particular SOCK_STREAM) and not of WebSockets. So why add the "Web" to "Sockets"? Why not simply build traditional Internet applications on top of TCP?

To answer this question, we need to distinguish between "unprivileged" and "privileged" application code. Unprivileged code is code running within a known origin, and is typically JavaScript running inside of a web page. In the Web security model, TCP connections cannot be safely opened by "unprivileged code." If unprivileged application code were allowed to open TCP connections, it would be possible for a script to originate HTTP requests with spoofed headers that falsely appear to come from a different origin. The ability to spoof headers in this way would make it pointless to have rules governing how scripts can make HTTP connections if the same scripts could sidestep those rules by re-implementing HTTP over TCP. Allowing TCP connections from web applications would break the origin model.

WebSocket connections formed from unprivileged code must therefore follow the same model as AJAX and other network capabilities allowed to unprivileged code. The HTTP handshake puts connection initialization under browser control and allows the browser to set the origin header and other headers that are necessary for preserving the origin model. This way, WebSocket allows applications to perform Internet-style networking with lightweight bidirectional connections while coexisting with HTTP applications, servers, and sandboxing rules.

WebSocket connections formed from privileged code can typically open any network connections; this ability isn't a problem (or at least, isn't a problem for the Web), because privileged apps have always been open to use any network connections and must be installed and executed by users. Native applications do not run in a web origin, so origin rules need not apply for WebSockets formed from privileged code.

Don't Confuse the User

In the past, one way to grant network access to unprivileged code was to prompt the user to grant selective permission to use the network when an application requested it. In theory, this method offers a solution to the same problems. When the user grants selective permission, the code could be allowed to make network connections when the user explicitly allowed it, though the application would put the responsibility of knowing how the application should behave on the user. In reality, users do not know the impact of granting permissions to code, and most users will blithely click OK. Users just want applications to work.

Security-related prompts are typically annoying, confusing, and often ignored, resulting in drastic consequences. The WebSocket approach denies applications from ever opening an unmediated TCP connection; however, it offers the same capabilities as typical networks, its security is better, and there is no user interface impact on the user because of origin. Origin lets the receiving server deny connections instead of asking the user to allow a connection.

Throttling New Connections

Although the origin header prevents floods of connections from being established at the HTTP layer, there is still a potential DoS threat from floods of connections opening at the TCP layer. Even open TCP connections carrying no data cost resources, and there is the potential for vast numbers of clients to overwhelm a server even with connections that the server would ultimately reject. To prevent connection overload, the WebSocket API requires browsers to throttle opening new connections. As you saw in Chapter 2, every call to the WebSocket constructor results in a new, open network socket. Browsers limit the rate at which underlying TCP sockets open, which in turn prevents floods of TCP connections from opening to hosts that will not accept them as WebSocket upgrades, and does not unduly slow down applications that legitimately want to open one or a small number of connections to the same host.

Headers with the "Sec-" Prefix

In the WebSocket opening handshake, there are several required HTTP headers, as you can see in Listings 7-1 and 7-2. Some of these headers are pervasive across the web platform, like origin, while other new headers were introduced to support WebSocket. The new headers were carefully chosen and named to prevent abuse of AJAX APIs to spoof WebSocket requests.

The client sends an HTTP request to the server asking to upgrade the protocol to WebSocket. If the server supports this upgrade, it responds with the corresponding headers. As explained in Chapter 3, some of these headers are required in order for the upgrade to complete successfully. Servers and browsers both enforce this exchange and acknowledgement of headers. Of these headers, some begin with the prefix "Sec-", and are described in RFC 6455. These headers are used in the opening WebSocket handshake (see Table 3-2 for a full description of these Sec- headers):

- Sec-WebSocket-Key

- Sec-WebSocket-Accept

- Sec-WebSocket-Extensions

- Sec-WebSocket-Protocol

- Sec-WebSocket-Version

Several header names are reserved by browsers for platform-level usage in the XMLHttpRequest specification and thus are off-limits for use in applications. These header names include those starting with Sec-, as well as common security-critical headers like referer, host, and cookie.

The new headers defined in RFC 6455 are all prefixed with Sec-. These prefixes are so named because the browser is opening WebSocket connections on behalf of applications, but the low-level, security sensitive parameters in the handshake are off-limits to application code. This effectively locks down upgrade requests so that they can only be made through APIs like the WebSocket constructor and not through general HTTP APIs like XMLHttpRequest.

WebSocket Secure Handshake: Accept Keys

You may recall from our discussion of the WebSocket Protocol that WebSocket connections succeed based on the server's response. The server must respond to the initial WebSocket handshake with the 101 response code, WebSocket upgrade header, and Sec-WebSocket-Accept header. The value of the Sec-WebSocket-Accept response header is derived from the Sec-WebSocket-Key request header and contains a special key response that must match exactly what the client expects.

The reason for the required exchange of the Sec-WebSocket-Key and Sec-WebSocket headers between the client and server is not obvious. The keys are only used during connection initialization, are easily intercepted, and clearly offer no protection to WebSocket clients or servers. What could these keys be protecting? These keys actually protect *non*-WebSocket servers and eliminate the possibility of cross-protocol attacks. Examples of cross-protocol attacks are those that make specially crafted WebSocket requests to non-WebSocket servers in order to establish connections or otherwise exploit them, and confuse servers expecting one protocol by making cleverly crafted connections with another protocol. To prevent cross protocol attacks using WebSocket, the handshake requires that the server transform a client-supplied key. If the server does not reply as expected, the client closes the connection. The WebSocket RFC contains a Globally Unique Identifier (GUID), which is a magic key used to identify the *protocol* rather than the connection or the user or any other participant in the system. The GUID is 258EAFA5-E914-47DA-95CA-C5AB0DC85B11.

The server reads the value of the Sec-WebSocket-Key header and performs the following steps:

1. Server adds GUID: 258EAFA5-E914-47DA-95CA-C5AB0DC85B11

2. Server transforms result with SHA1 hash

3. Server transforms result with Base64 encoding

4. Server sends result back as the value of the Sec-WebSocket-Accept header

By performing a specific transformation of the provided key, the server proves that it specifically understands the WebSocket Protocol, as a server that doesn't know the hash isn't really a WebSocket server. This transformation heads off direct cross-protocol attacks, because real WebSocket clients and servers will insist on only talking among themselves.

HTTP Proxies and Masking

In Chapters 2 and 3, we discussed WebSocket frames, which comprise WebSocket messages. WebSocket frames sent from browsers to servers are masked to obfuscate the frames' contents, because intercepting proxy servers can be confused by WebSocket traffic. In Chapter 3, we discussed how masking WebSocket frames improves compatibility with existing HTTP proxies. There is, however, another, rather unusual and subtle reason for masking that has to do with security.

Unlike regular HTTP request-response traffic, WebSocket connections can remain open for a long time. In older architectures, proxy servers are configured to allow such connections and can handle the traffic gracefully, but they can also interfere with WebSocket traffic and cause headaches.

A proxy server acts as an intermediary between a client and another server, is often used to monitor traffic, and can sometimes close a connection if it has been open too long. Proxy servers may choose to close long-lived WebSocket connections because the proxy server sees the connections as trying to connect with an unresponsive HTTP server.

Figure 7-2 shows a simple example of a network topology with WebSocket, proxy servers, and web applications. Here, client applications in a browser access back-end TCP-based services using a WebSocket connection. Some of these clients are located inside a corporate intranet, protected by a corporate firewall and configured to access the Web through explicit proxy servers (see Figure 7-2); these proxy servers may cache content and provide some level of security. Other client applications access a WebSocket server directly. In both cases, the client requests may be routed through transparent proxy servers.

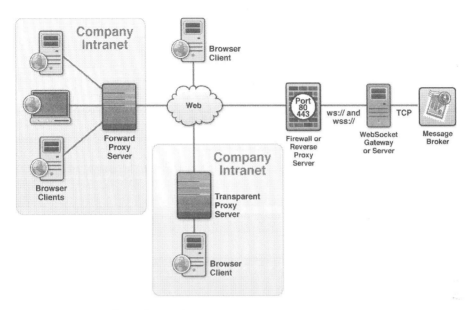

Figure 7-2. *Network topology with proxy servers*

Figure 7-2 shows three types of proxy servers:

- Forward proxy server: Typically installed, configured, and controlled by the server administrator. A forward proxy server directs outgoing requests from an intranet to the Internet.

- Reverse proxy server: Typically installed, configured, and controlled by the server administrator. A reverse proxy server (or firewall) is typically deployed in a network DMZ in front of the server and performs security functions to protect internal servers from incoming attacks from the Internet.

- Transparent proxy server: Typically controlled by a network operator. A transparent proxy server typically intercepts network communication for caching or preventing company intranet users from accessing the Web for specific purpose. Network operators may use a transparent proxy server to cache commonly accessed websites to reduce network load.

All these intercepting proxy servers can be confused by WebSocket traffic, which can be especially true with transparent proxy servers. For example, attackers may poison an HTTP cache on a transparent proxy server. HTTP cache poisoning is a type of attack in which an attacker exercises control over an HTTP cache to serve dangerous content in place of the requested resources. Cache poisoning became a major issue during the standardization of WebSocket after a group of researchers wrote a paper outlining a theoretical attack on transparent intercepting proxies using HTTP upgrade requests. This paper, *Talking to Yourself for Fun and Profit* (Huang, Chen, Barth, Rescorla, & Jackson, 2011) convinced the working group that WebSocket was dangerous to standardize without some protection against these possible attacks. How could poisoning be prevented? After much contentious debate by the working group, masking was added to the WebSocket Protocol. Masking is a technique for obscuring (but not encrypting) the protocol contents to prevent confusion in transparent intercepting proxies. As discussed in Chapter 3, masking transforms the payload of each message sent from browsers to WebSocket servers by XORing the contents with a few random bytes.

Previously, we mentioned that plugins and extensions can open sockets if they request permission, and that installed applications use network connections with arbitrary traffic all the time. What's stopping someone behind such a proxy from opening a terminal and crafting that kind of network traffic manually? The answer is: nothing at all. Masking does not fix the problems in the proxies, though it does not exacerbate an existing problem. On the Web, where applications are not installed and you run thousands of scripts from different sources simply by browsing around, everything is magnified. Web APIs have to be more paranoid.

Like origin, masking is a security feature that does not need to be cryptographically secure against eavesdropping. Both ends and any middlemen can understand the masked payload if they desire. However, for middlemen who do not understand the masked payload, they are critically protected from misinterpreting the content of WebSocket messages as HTTP requests and responses.

Secure WebSocket Uses TLS (You Should, Too!)

As we discussed in Chapter 3, the WebSocket Protocol defines WebSocket (ws://) and WebSocket Secure (wss://) prefixes; both connections use the HTTP upgrade mechanism to upgrade to the WebSocket Protocol. Transport Layer Security (TLS) is the protocol used when accessing secure websites with a URL that begins with https://. TLS protects data during transit and verifies its authenticity. WebSocket Secure connections are secured by tunneling through TLS using the WebSocket Secure (WSS) URL scheme wss://. By securing WebSocket communication with TLS, you protect the confidentiality, integrity, and availability of your network communications. In this chapter, we focus on confidentiality and integrity as they pertain to WebSocket security, and explore the benefits of TLS from a deployment standpoint in Chapter 8.

▨ **Note** TLS has its own RFC defined by the IETF: http://tools.ietf.org/html/rfc5246.

You can use a plain, unencrypted WebSocket connection (prefixed by ws://) for testing or even simple topologies. If you are deploying a service on a network, the benefits of wire-level encryption are enormous and the drawbacks are relatively small.

The major historical drawbacks of using encryption on the Web have all been greatly reduced with enhancements to the TLS protocol and modern machines. In the past, you might have chosen not to use HTTPS due to high CPU cost, lack of virtual hosting, and slow startup times for new connections. These concerns are now allayed with modern improvements.

There are some pleasant side effects of deploying TLS, as well. Encrypted WebSocket traffic generally works more smoothly through proxies. Encryption prevents proxies from inspecting traffic, so they generally just let the bytes through without attempting to buffer or change the traffic flow. See Chapter 8 for more information about deploying encrypted WebSocket services.

Just like WebSocket begins with an HTTP handshake before upgrading to WebSocket, the WebSocket Secure (WSS) handshake begins with an HTTPS handshake. The HTTPS and WSS protocols are very similar, with both running on top of TLS over TCP connections. You configure TLS encryption for WebSocket wire traffic the same way you do for HTTP: using certificates. With HTTPS, the client and server first establish a secure connection and only then begins the HTTP protocol. Similarly, WSS establishes a secure connection, begins the HTTP handshake, and then upgrades to the WebSocket wire protocol. The benefit of this is that if you know how to configure HTTPS for encrypted communication, then you also know how to configure WSS for encrypted WebSocket communication.

The cables at the top of the Figure 7-3 show how HTTPS is not a separate protocol, rather the combination of HTTP running on a TLS connection. Commonly, HTTPS uses a different port than HTTP (HTTPS's default port is 443 and HTTP's default port is 80). HTTP runs directly on TCP and HTTPS runs on TLS, which, in turn, runs on TCP.

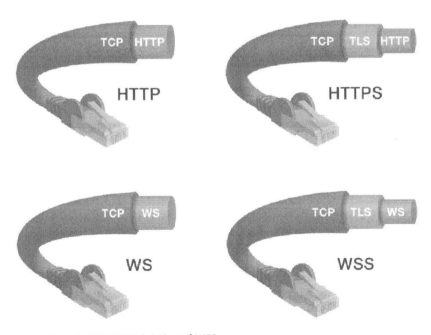

Figure 7-3. *HTTP, HTTPS, WS, and WSS*

The cables at the bottom of the figure show that the same is true for WebSocket Secure (WSS) connectivity. The WebSocket (WS) protocol runs on TCP (like HTTP), and the WSS connection runs on TLS, which, in turn, runs on TCP. The WebSocket Protocol is compatible with HTTP such that the WebSocket connection uses the same ports: the WebSocket default port is 80 and WebSocket Secure (WSS) uses port 443 by default.

Authentication

To confirm the identity of users connecting to our servers via WebSocket, WebSocket handshakes can include cookie headers. Using cookie headers allows servers to use the same cookies for WebSocket authentication that are used to authenticate HTTP requests.

At the time of writing this book, browsers do not allow other forms of HTTP authentication from the WebSocket API. Interestingly, the API does not disallow these mechanisms; they just won't work with browsers. If a server responds to a WebSocket upgrade request with status 401 Authentication Required, for instance, the browser will simply close the WebSocket connection. The assumption in this model is that users will have already logged into an application via HTTP before that application attempts to open a WebSocket connection.

Alternatively, authentication could take place over the application layer protocol after the WebSocket upgrade has completed. Protocols such as XMPP and STOMP have semantics for identifying users and exchanging credentials built into those layers. One could deploy unauthenticated WebSockets but require authentication at the next protocol layer. In the following section, Application Level Security, we discuss how authorization can be enforced at the application protocol level, as well.

Application Level Security

Application Level Security dictates how applications can protect themselves from attacks that may expose private information. This level of security protects the resources exposed by the application. You can take advantage of application level security on your WebSocket-based system if you are using a standard protocol such as XMPP, STOMP, or Advanced Message Queueing Protocol (AMQP). Configuring permissions is specific to the server.

In Chapter 5, we used the Apache ActiveMQ message broker to illustrate how to build applications using STOMP over WebSocket. Here, we'll continue to build upon the ActiveMQ configuration and restrict access to its resources, and we'll do so by implementing security to the sample WebSocket application that ships with Apache ActiveMQ.

In this section, we review two application security measures. First, we take a look at a simple authentication plugin that requires users to authenticate themselves before accessing ActiveMQ. Then, we take a look at how to configure authorization to protect specific queues and topics.

Before we get started, let's make sure that you can access the demo without providing credentials to ensure you don't already have application authentication and authorization configured. Using the following command, start ActiveMQ:

```
$> bin/activemq console
```

Navigate to the ActiveMQ welcome page, by default located at `http://0.0.0.0:8161/`. Click the *See some web demos* link, and open the WebSocket example. The default URL for this demo is: `http://0.0.0.0:8161/demo/websocket/index.html`.

Modify the host name in the Server URL field from `localhost` to `0.0.0.0`, and click Connect. As Figure 7-4 indicates, you should now be connected.

Figure 7-4. *Apache ActiveMQ configured with no authentication*

Since ActiveMQ isn't configured to perform authentication, any credentials you enter are simply ignored. You can confirm this behavior by changing the Login and Password fields to arbitrary values, then clicking Connect again. You should still be able to connect. Now, let's add authentication to our application.

Application Authentication

When configured, authentication blocks users from accessing ActiveMQ, unless they provide the right credentials. Let's review how to configure authentication and how you can define the credentials for your users.

Listing 7-3 shows a sample configuration snippet that you can add to the configuration we used in Chapter 5. When you add this to the `conf/activemq.xml` file in the Apache ActiveMQ installation directory, you restrict user access to the system and ActiveMQ challenges the user with a username and a password.

▓ **Note**   You can define various configuration files for Apache ActiveMQ. To keep our example simple, here we modify the default one. For additional Apache ActiveMQ configurations, see the ACTIVEMQ_HOME/conf directory.

Listing 7-3. Sample Apache ActiveMQ Configuration

```
<plugins>
        <simpleAuthenticationPlugin>
                    <users>
                           <authenticationUser username="system"
        password="${activemq.password}"
                                 groups="users,admins"/>
                           <authenticationUser username="user"
        password="${guest.password}"
                                 groups="users"/>
                           <authenticationUser username="guest"
        password="${guest.password}" groups="guests"/>
                    </users>
        </simpleAuthenticationPlugin>
</plugins>
```

Listing 7-3 is available as a sample in the conf/activemq-security.xml file, as well.

Let's start the Apache ActiveMQ message broker with the new configuration. In the ACTIVEMQ_HOME directory enter the following:

```
$> bin/activemq console
```

Now, when you try to access the sample application with the same username and password provided by the demo causes the system to reject the user's login as shown in Figure 7-5. The reason for this is that the value of the pre-populated value of the Login and Password fields is guest, by default, while the configuration you just added refers to the ${guest.password} property, as specified in the ACTIVEMQ_HOME/conf/credentials.properties file.

Figure 7-5 content (screenshot of Apache ActiveMQ web interface showing the STOMP websocket demo form with Server URL, Login, Password, Destination fields, a Connect button, and an error log output showing a SecurityException for invalid user name/password)

Figure 7-5. *Apache ActiveMQ rejects user login with new configuration*

Providing the right username and password combination will let the user access the system. The default password for the guest user is `password` (as defined in `ACTIVEMQ_HOME/conf/credentials.properties`).

Listing 7-4 shows a line in the authentication plugin configuration that tells the Apache ActiveMQ message broker that the user `guest` has his or her own password and that the user is part of the `guests` group.

Listing 7-4. Setting a Password and Group for User Guest

```
<authenticationUser username="guest" password="${guest.password}"
groups="guests"/>
```

Application Authorization

After successful authentication, you want to grant access to certain application resources, while denying access to some others. In this section, we review what you need to do to grant users and groups access to specific queues and topics.

Listing 7-5 shows a configuration that, when added to the ACTIVEMQ_HOME/conf/activemq.xml file, restricts deliberate access to the message broker destinations. The configuration shows how to enable or disable access to the users depending on the application requirements. Similar to the authentication snippet, the authorizationPlugin must be surrounded by the <plugins> tag. The order of authorization and authentication within the plugins tag is not relevant.

Listing 7-5. Restricting Deliberate Access to the Message Broker Destinations

```
<authorizationPlugin>
   <map>
     <authorizationMap>
       <authorizationEntries>
          <authorizationEntry queue=">" read="admins"write="admins"
admin="admins" />
          <authorizationEntry queue="USERS.>" read="users" write="users"
admin="users" />
          <authorizationEntry queue="GUEST.>" read="guests"
write="guests,users" admin="guests,users" />

          <authorizationEntry queue="TEST.Q" read="guests" write="guests" />

          <authorizationEntry topic=">" read="admins" write="admins"
admin="admins" />
          <authorizationEntry topic="USERS.>" read="users" write="users"
admin="users" />
          <authorizationEntry topic="GUEST.>" read="guests"
write="guests,users" admin="guests,users" />

          <authorizationEntry topic="ActiveMQ.Advisory.>" read="guests,
users" write="guests,users" admin="guests,users"/>
       </authorizationEntries>
     </authorizationMap>
   </map>
</authorizationPlugin>
```

The sample configuration in Listing 7-5 specifies that admins have full access to all the queues and topics, while guests have access only to queues and topics that have a GUEST. prefix in their name.

Restart ActiveMQ to pick up the configuration changes. When you reload the sample demo application in the web browser, be sure to change the default password to the value of password, then click Connect. The user will be authenticated but will not be able to send or receive messages, as the topic name doesn't have the right prefix.

Figure 7-6 shows that the user can connect to the system but cannot send to the test queue.

Figure 7-6. User successfully connects but cannot send messages

Now, set the Destination field to /queue/GUEST.test, then click Connect. Figure 7-7 shows the result of the successful login and that the user is now authorized to send and receive messages on this queue.

145

Figure 7-7. User successfully connects and is authorized to receive messages

The user is now able to send and receive messages because you set an authorization policy in the ActiveMQ configuration to let users, part of the *guests* group to read, write, and manage any queues and topics that are prefixed with GUEST. Listing 7-6 shows the authorization policy.

Listing 7-6. Authorization Policy in ActiveMQ

```
<authorizationEntry queue="GUEST.>" read="guests" write="guests,users"
admin="guests,users" />
```

■ **Note**   Apache ActiveMQ makes use of destination wildcards providing support for federated name hierarchies.

As you can see, you can control security for your application simply by configuring your back-end message broker. Enhancing security on your application resources further tightens the security model over WebSocket, from your back-end server over WebSocket, all the way to the application in the browser.

146

Summary

Security is an extremely important aspect of Web application deployment, and is no less important with WebSocket applications. In this chapter, we examined areas of Web security that pertain to WebSocket, and how to address them with commonly used security protocols like TLS, features built into WebSocket like masking, and the origin header, whose definition was refined specifically for the WebSocket specification. Finally, we stepped through an example of how you can implement application-level security through application authentication and authorization to protect resources at the source.

In the next chapter, we'll further explore security as it relates to deployment, as well as discuss considerations you need to make when you decide to deploy your WebSocket application to the Web.

CHAPTER 8

▓ ▓ ▓

Deployment Considerations

After you've built, secured, and tested any web application, the next logical step is to deploy it. Many considerations you must make when deploying WebSocket applications are similar to those of any web application. In this chapter, we focus on the areas of web application deployment that you should think about when deploying WebSocket applications in particular.

When deploying an application, there are myriad factors you must consider, especially for enterprises, such as business requirements, how clients will interact with the application, the information the application uses, the number of clients that will use the application at any given time, and so on. Some applications may require high availability and must support many concurrent connections, while others may have a stronger emphasis on performance and low latency. With WebSocket applications, you'll need to provide for the same requirements, keeping in mind the nature of the WebSocket Protocol and the type of application you're building. In this chapter, we'll look at some of the major aspects of deployment as they specifically relate to WebSocket, like WebSocket emulation, proxies and firewalls, load balancing, and capacity planning.

Overview of WebSocket Application Deployment

When deploying any web application, there are some general requirements you need to take into account, such as the variety of browsers that will be using your application, the type of application, the nature of the traffic your servers must handle, and whether the application is driven by the server or by user interaction. Now that your mind is exploding with all sorts of new applications you can build with WebSocket, you'll need to take these application requirements into consideration when deploying them.

For example, you can imagine a WebSocket-based messaging application (using STOMP over WebSocket, as we described in Chapter 5) where your application must support thousands—nay, tens of thousands—concurrent connections. Your application may be a stock portfolio application, where your users can track the millions of stock transactions that happen daily. This data must refresh instantly and in real time in order for the application to be useful; as such, you may be looking at a system where the full-duplex connection is used by the server to stream continuous stock information to the user's browser or mobile device, with little user interaction. In another case, you may want to use WebSocket to create a customizable video streaming application, where large amounts of data (several minute-long video files) may stream over the connection, but to just a few thousand clients at time; this traffic may be sporadic throughout the day, with peaks during certain times of the day, and with heavy interaction by users requesting, sharing, and posting videos. Each scenario is ideal for WebSocket, and each has different deployment requirements.

In the earlier chapters of this book, you also learned about different ways you can use standard protocols over WebSocket. One of the choices you can make, which you learned in Chapter 4, is that you can choose to enable WebSocket in your server (for example, you could enable your XMPP chat server to speak WebSocket) or choose to use a gateway that sits between your TCP-based server and your clients, but enables you to layer standard protocols over WebSocket to take advantage of the full-duplex connection. In each of these cases, you may need to think about how your WebSocket-enabled back-end server or your WebSocket gateway will handle a variety of client connections.

The difference between *application deployment* and *WebSocket application deployment* is not vast, but there are some areas to think about when deploying your WebSocket application.

WebSocket Emulation and Fallback

While modern browsers natively support WebSocket, there are still many older versions of browsers without native WebSocket support that are widely used, many of which are in corporate environments or under business requirements that strictly control browsers and versions. As a developer, you often do not have control over the type of browser used to access your application, but you still want to accommodate as wide an audience as possible. There are ways to achieve "emulation" of WebSocket's capabilities by using other communication strategies between cooperating client libraries and servers. There is also the option to fall back to another communication technique as a last resort.

Plugins

One way you can establish full-duplex communication is with plugins. A common plugin is Adobe Flash, which lets you open a TCP socket. While Flash tends to be installed in most desktop browsers, if it is not present, users must explicitly download it, which can be intrusive to the user experience. Using a plugin for communication also impacts the performance of your application due to the expensive communication between Flash and your application code. Even worse, using Flash sockets can cause your application to hang for up to three seconds while connecting. Also, keep in mind that Adobe Flash is not fully supported in the popular iOS, Android, and Windows RT environments. This lack of support means plugin-based fallback strategies are becoming less and less viable as browsers continue to move away from plugin-based extensibility.

Polyfills

A viable alternative to plugins is a polyfill, which is a library that implements a standard API using legacy browser features. Polyfills allow developers to target new web standards while creating applications and still reach users with older browsers. A number of polyfills exist for a variety of HTML5 features, including graphics, forms, and databases. Polyfills can use multiple strategies to implement a standard API. For example, Kaazing has a polyfill for the WebSocket API that uses secret sauce streaming techniques and provides a fallback solution for WebSocket applications running on browsers that do not support WebSocket.

Modernizr, an open source project for HTML5 best practices, maintains a wiki with an up-to-date list of polyfills and their descriptions for a wide array of HTML5 technologies, including WebSocket at `https://github.com/Modernizr/Modernizr/wiki/HTML5-Cross-Browser-Polyfills`.

Different Abstraction Layers

There are other libraries like Socket.io that use WebSocket and Comet techniques to expose a single API. Some of these libraries have APIs that are the same as the standard WebSocket API, and therefore are polyfills. Other libraries include APIs that differ from the WebSocket API, but use WebSocket as a transport strategy to provide a different communication abstraction. This technique does not necessarily make them less optimal than polyfills, but code written against standard interfaces is more portable and future proof in anticipation of the day when fallback libraries are no longer necessary.

Even the best fallback implementations that employ Comet techniques have their downsides. These are, essentially, the flipside of the benefits of using WebSocket as a transport layer protocol in your applications. Emulation is essential for ensuring connectivity with legacy browsers and over adverse networks, but it is important to know what you are losing when you resort to a fallback strategy. Many of the reasons are what compelled WebSocket to be developed in the first place. When choosing and designing your fallback strategy, you may want to keep in mind that these emulation techniques:

- **Are Non-Standard:** As we described in Chapter 1, these fallback options are non-standard, which was one of the reasons WebSocket was created. With these non-standard techniques, different WebSocket emulation clients and servers cannot communicate among themselves.

- **Provide Decreased Performance:** High performance Comet implementations can stream data in only one direction: from the server to the browser. Even optimal WebSocket emulation over AJAX implementations cannot stream data from browsers to servers.

- **Have Browser Connection Limits:** Browsers restrict the number of HTTP connections per host. Comet connections count against this limit.

- **Have Complicated (or Non-Functional) Cross-Origin Deployment:** WebSocket has had origin security built in from day one. Cross-origin AJAX requires additional configuration to work with legacy browsers, when it works at all.

Proxies and Other Network Intermediaries

In Chapter 7, we discussed proxy servers and how they relate to WebSocket security. Proxies fall into the category of "middleboxes," which are network intermediaries that sit between your web applications and servers.

There are two distinct classes of middleboxes that can impact deployment: intermediaries that sit between your servers and the Internet, and intermediaries that sit between your users and the Internet. On the server side, you or your organization typically controls firewalls and reverse proxies that are part of your server infrastructure. These server-side intermediaries are added in order to support your infrastructure or enforce security policies.

On the client side, users are frequently behind firewalls and forward proxies. Their connections pass through these intermediaries on the way out to the network. With the exception of some closed environments, you cannot control the networks used to connect to your servers. You can, however, make decisions when deploying your WebSocket servers that can make connections through those networks smoother and more frequently successful.

When considering deploying your WebSocket application, you'll want to take into account the various possible intermediaries that can handle traffic between your clients and servers.

Reverse Proxies and Load Balancing

Reverse proxies are specific types of servers that accept web client connections on behalf of one or more servers. There are several uses for reverse proxies including hiding the existence and characteristics of the origin servers, application firewall, TLS (or SSL) termination and offloading, load balancing, caching static content, and enabling dynamic content through WebSocket. Reverse proxies can also be used whenever multiple web servers must be accessible from a single public IP address and port.

Figure 8-1 shows a simple topology with reverse proxy server in front of an HTTP server and a WebSocket server.

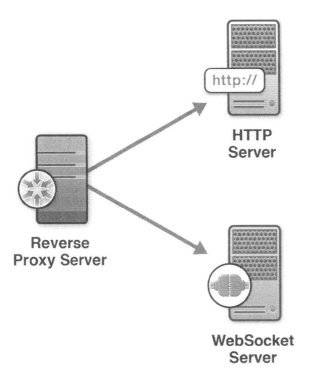

Figure 8-1. *Reverse Proxy Server in Front of HTTP and WebSocket Servers*

Using a reverse proxy server provides several benefits, including enabling you to deploy, administer, and update your WebSocket server separately from other servers in your network. While reverse proxy servers can enable your application to use a single port to access the servers in your topology, as the number of users increase, you'll need to consider load-balancing options. For example, you may have an HTTP server serving static content and multiple WebSocket servers serving dynamic content for your web application.

You can use a reverse proxy as a load balancer in front of your servers by configuring the proxy server to balance the load among a number of WebSocket servers. For example, you can create a network of HTTP and WebSocket servers by using the reverse proxy server to point to ws1.example.com, ws2.example.com, and so on, as shown in Figure 8-2.

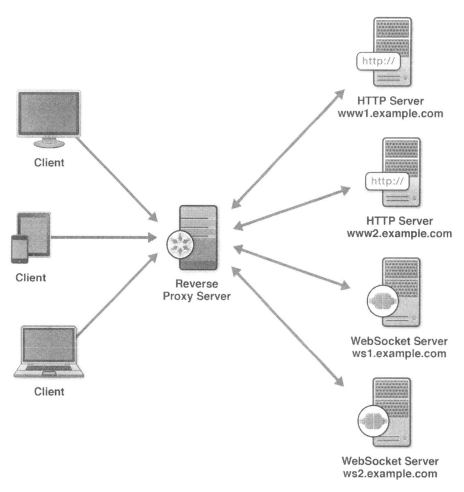

Figure 8-2. *Reverse proxy server as a load balancer*

REVERSE CONNECTIVITY

Reverse proxy servers connect to servers inside your secure network in order to establish end-to-end communication. Sometimes, the back-end server you would like to use cannot receive connections, which commonly occurs in two situations: during early development when you want to allow connections to a WebSocket server running on localhost or on a local network, and in some enterprise deployments, where application servers are behind a firewall that prevents all incoming connections (usually for security reasons and/or the policy of your organization).

You may recall our discussion about addressability in Chapter 3, where we identified a fundamental problem: some machines on the Internet can only make outgoing connections and cannot be directly addressed. WebSocket essentially solves this problem for web clients, which cannot be directly accessed by servers. Servers can only send newly available data to a client on a connection that was initiated by that client. By keeping a persistent connection open from web clients, WebSocket removes this limitation. Similarly, reverse connectivity or tunneling keeps a persistent connection open from WebSocket servers. Reverse connectivity for servers uses persistent connections from non-addressable hosts to publicly available endpoints. The publicly available endpoint forwards connections over this persistent tunnel to servers that would otherwise be unable to accept connections. If your WebSocket server does not have a public address, you may want to use reverse connectivity to make it available.

Traverse Proxies and Firewalls with Transport Layer Security (TLS or SSL)

Throughout this book, we've mentioned Transport Layer Security (TLS, formerly known as SSL) frequently for an important reason. TLS hides network traffic from inspection and interference by man-in-the-middle attackers. TLS helps connections flow smoothly through some kinds of common web proxies, as well. In this section, we look at the effects of different types of proxy on WebSocket connections. Hopefully, by the end of this section, you'll see why we recommend deploying WebSocket over TLS, even when it is not a security requirement.

Because forward proxies manage traffic between private networks and the Internet, they can also close a connection if it has been open for too long. This expected action by a proxy server represents a risk to technologies, like WebSocket, that require persistent connections. We discuss how to offset this with pings and pongs later in this chapter. Proxies are also more likely to buffer unencrypted HTTP responses, thereby introducing unpredictable latency during HTTP response streaming.

Without any intermediary servers, a WebSocket connection can be established smoothly, as long as both understand the WebSocket Protocol. However, with the proliferation of network intermediaries between you and the Internet, there are cases that you need to understand when deploying your WebSocket-based application, as described in Table 8-1.

Table 8-1. *Using Encrypted/Unencrypted WebSocket with Explicit and Transparent Proxy Servers*

Proxy Server Type	WebSocket Connection	Connection Result	Considerations
No proxy	Unencrypted and Encrypted	Connection succeeds	WebSocket connections succeed if there are no network intermediaries between the client and the server.
Explicit	Unencrypted	Connection succeeds* *Only if the proxy server correctly ignores traffic after the CONNECT method	An explicit proxy server allows the CONNECT method. The resulting connection is non-secure.
Explicit	Encrypted	Connection succeeds	An explicit proxy server allows the CONNECT method. The client sends the TLS handshake, followed by the WebSocket connection upgrade handshake. After this series of handshakes succeeds, WebSocket traffic can start flowing unimpeded through the proxy server.
Transparent	Unencrypted	Connection fails	A well-behaved transparent proxy server does not understand the 101 response code, and thus should cause the WebSocket handshake to fail almost immediately.
Transparent	Encrypted	Connection succeeds	Because the traffic is encrypted, a transparent proxy allows the connection to succeed and the WebSocket traffic to flow.

Proxies are often grouped into two categories: explicit and transparent proxies. The proxy server is explicit when the browser is explicitly configured to use it. For explicit proxies you have to provide your browser with the proxy's host name, port number, and optionally user name and password. The proxy server is transparent when the browser is not aware that the traffic is intercepted by a proxy.

Using WebSocket Secure (WSS) increases the odds that connections will succeed even when there are middleboxes on the network performing transparent inspection and modification of outgoing connections.

Figure 8-3 further illustrates the cases where the WebSocket connection may or may not succeed depending on a combination of variables such as plain WebSocket Protocol vs. WebSocket Secure and explicit proxy configuration as well as transparent proxy servers.

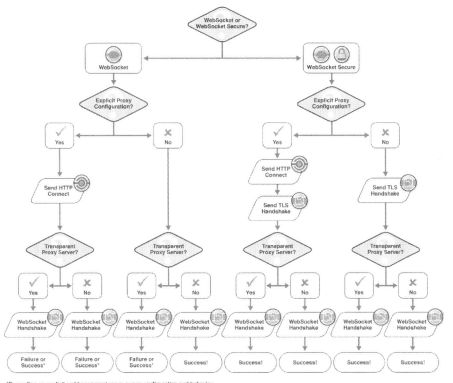

Figure 8-3. *How WebSocket interacts with proxy servers*

As you can see in Figure 8-3, using WSS can dramatically increase the chances that your WebSocket connection will succeed, even when the traffic has to traverse explicit and transparent proxies.

Deploying TLS

Deploying TLS requires cryptographic digital certificates that are used to identify WebSocket servers. In production environments, these certificates must be signed by a certificate authority (CA) that is known and trusted by web browsers. If you use an untrusted certificate, users will see security errors when accessing your server, which is how TLS prevents man-in-the-middle attacks from hijacking connections as they open. During development, you can sign your own certificates and configure your browser to trust those certificates and ignore the security warnings.

WebSocket Pings and Pongs

Connections can unexpectedly close for many reasons beyond your control. Any web application should be coded to gracefully deal with intermittent connectivity and recover appropriately. There are, however, reasons connections close that can and should be avoided. One common cause of connectivity loss that *is* avoidable is inactivity at the TCP level, which in turn affects WebSocket connections.

■ **Note**   Because WebSocket connections are layered on top of TCP connections, connection issues that occur at the TCP level affect WebSocket connections.

With a full-duplex connection between your client and WebSocket server, there may be times when there is no data flowing over the connection. At that point, a network intermediary may terminate the connection. Specifically, network components that are not aware of "always on" connections sometimes close down inactive TCP, and therefore WebSocket, connections. For example, proxy servers and home routers sometimes terminate what they perceive as idle connections. The WebSocket Protocol supports pings and pongs both to perform health checks on the connection and to keep the connection open.

Using WebSocket pings and pongs keeps the connection open and ready for data flow. Pings and pongs can originate from either side of an open WebSocket connection. The WebSocket Protocol supports client-initiated and server-initiated pings and pongs. The browser or server can send pings, pongs, or both at appropriate intervals to keep connections active. Note that we've said browser, and not WebSocket client: as we mentioned in Chapter 2, the WebSocket API does not currently support client-initiated pings and pongs. While the browser may send pings and pongs according to its own keep-alive and health-check policies, most pings and pongs are going to be server-initiated; the WebSocket client can then respond to pings with a pong. Alternatively, the browser or server can send pongs without receiving a ping, which gives you flexibility in keeping your connections alive. The exact intervals you use depend on the audience for your application and the normal rate of data flowing over your application's WebSocket connections. Conservatively, sending a pong every thirty seconds ought to keep most connections alive, but sending pongs less frequently saves bandwidth and server resources.

WebSocket Buffering and Throttling

With WebSocket applications using full-duplex connections, you can control the rate at which applications send data to the server, also known as "throttling." Throttling the traffic can help avoid saturation or bottlenecks in the network that may be influenced by other limitations, such as Internet bandwidth and server CPU limits, which we'll discuss in the subsequent sections. The WebSocket API enables you to control the rate that the applications send data to the server, with the WebSocket bufferedAmount attribute, which we discussed in Chapter 2. The bufferedAmount attribute represents the number of bytes that have been queued but not transmitted to the server yet.

You can also throttle client connections to the server and allow the server to determine whether to accept or reject the client connection depending on pre-defined settings in the server.

Monitoring

To assess your system's performance, you can also configure a monitoring tool to track user activity, server performance, and terminate client sessions, if necessary. Monitoring is extremely useful not only in analyzing the health of your network and system, but also in diagnosing the root cause of performance bottlenecks or failures and identifying areas where you can tune aspects of the system for better performance.

Ideally, you should be able to provide visibility and control needed to assure that business transactions are flowing through the system without any issues and meeting the service-level agreements (SLAs).

Capacity Planning

Implementing WebSocket in your architecture enables you to build flexible and scalable frameworks. Even with this flexibility, you must still plan for the needs of the deployment, including sizing considerations, specifically in relation to hardware capacity. Among these areas are the memory and CPU of the server (whether it's your back-end server that has been WebSocket-enabled or a gateway that enables WebSocket traffic to flow between clients and back-end servers), and network optimization. In general, *sizing* means estimating the hardware requirements for your application.

Table 8-2 describes areas you may want to take into account when thinking about the hardware requirements for your WebSocket application. The items in this checklist contain factors to consider when deploying any application and may certainly change over time as your user base, data, and system grow.

Table 8-2. *Capacity Planning Checklist*

Planning Item	Notes
Message Size	Identify the typical size of data your WebSocket server will send to your clients.
Frequency	Identify the rate of message delivery. For example, whether your application requires slow delivery (such as human-generated chat messages) or rapid delivery (such as machine-generated messages like up-to-date positioning of multiple airplanes).
Concurrency	Identify the number of clients that will connect to your server at the same time.
Data Duplication	Determine whether all (or most) clients receive the same data or if each client receives unique data.
Software Configuration	Identify limitations or possible performance enhancements from the server software (for example, the Java Virtual Machine).
Memory	Determine memory requirements based on message size and delivery rate.
Network	• Identify the network requirements for the network interface card (NIC), as well as the requirements if you're using virtual server with software NICs. • Identify the bandwidth and latency requirements for your servers' connections to the Internet.
User Expectations	Determine how the user will use the application, such as whether information transmitted to one device must be continually updated on all the user's devices.

Alternatively, there are a number of cloud-based WebSocket service offerings available that essentially eliminate the need for a WebSocket developer to consider capacity planning. The service providers take responsibility for ensuring sufficient capacity is available to their customers, allowing the elastic scaling of the deployed applications.

Socket Limits

As you know, WebSocket servers hold many connections open at the same time. You should be aware that if you run a server without changing any operating system settings, you probably would not be able to maintain more than a few thousand open sockets. You'll see errors reporting that you cannot open any more files, even if there are plenty of CPU and memory resources available. (Remember, in UNIX, just about everything is a file, including sockets! You could see an error message about files, even if you aren't using the disk.) Operating systems limit the number of open files per user; by default, this limit is fairly low. These limits are in place to prevent abuse on shared systems where many users have to contend for the same resources. On a server, however, you likely want to allow one process to run full-throttle and use as many open files as it can.

For example, on Linux, the command `ulimit -a` displays the current user limits, including the maximum allowable number of open files. You can fortunately raise this limit on Linux (for example, you can run `ulimit -n 10000` to set the user limit to ten thousand open files). There is also a system-wide maximum, `fs.file-max`, that you can raise using the `sysctl` command. These commands might not be the same for your operating system, as file limits are dependent on the operating system. For example, on Microsoft Windows, the commands vary by version; in some cases, you cannot modify the limit. Consult the references for your system in order to set the maximum number of open sockets for your WebSocket server.

WebSocket Application Deployment Checklist

Table 8-3 is a checklist that summarizes considerations for deploying WebSocket applications.

Table 8-3. *WebSocket Application Deployment Checklist*

Planning Item	Notes
WebSocket Emulation and Fallback	• Identify your users' browsers and versions. • Determine if a fallback strategy is necessary. If so, employ polyfill, plugin, or Comet fallbacks.
Reverse Proxy and Load Balancing	• Identify the port(s) you want to open to the public. • Identify the servers with which the reverse proxy must operate. • Determine whether you can open a port in your firewall, and therefore whether you should use reverse connectivity. • Identify the load requirements of your network resources, including servers and client connections.
Traversing Proxies and Firewalls with TLS	• Identify proxies and firewalls that may disrupt your WebSocket traffic. • Decide to use TLS for security and/or connectivity reasons.
Keep Alive	• Identify the connections you want to monitor. • Set ping intervals to prevent connection timeout.

(continued)

Table 8-3. (*continued*)

Planning Item	Notes
Buffering and Throttling	Identify where throttling may improve performance.
Monitoring	Identify areas for monitoring.
Hardware Capacity Planning	• Identify the memory and CPU requirements for your WebSocket server.
	• Identify bandwidth requirements.
	• Identify the disk requirements of your servers.
	• Decide if a cloud-based offering would better suit your application deployment.
Socket Limits	• Identify the number of concurrent socket connections your system requirements.
	• Identify the socket limits for your server.

Summary

In this chapter, we examined the steps you can take after you've built your WebSocket server and application and added the necessary security enhancements to prepare your application for public consumption. We looked at some of the tasks an application developer can perform to allow all types of users to access their WebSocket application, even if the user does not have a WebSocket-enabled browser. We explored ways you can work with reverse proxy servers and TCP keepalive to maintain WebSocket connections, use TLS to protect your data (not only from intruders but also from proxies and firewalls), as well as plan for enterprise-wide deployment.

You've now walked with us through the history of the WebSocket API and Protocol and examined the benefits of using WebSocket over older HTTP architectures. We've looked at sample WebSocket traffic and through this examination witnessed the possibilities of improved performance. We've stepped through using the WebSocket API and seen how much simpler it is to create full-duplex, bidirectional communication between a client and server than with older (and more convoluted) AJAX-based architectures. We explored some of the powerful ways you can use WebSocket to extend TCP layer application protocols over the Web with widely used standards, like XMPP and STOMP. With these use cases, we've seen how you can empower standard chat and messaging protocols with full-duplex, real-time capabilities. We've seen how you can easily implement desktop sharing using VNC over WebSocket to a plugin-free HTML5 browser client. We've also looked at security and deployment for WebSocket applications, and considerations you should make before making your applications publicly available.

After reading *The Definitive Guide to HTML5 WebSocket*, we hope you are not only armed with a good understanding of WebSocket but are also inspired to take advantage of this technology to ramp up your existing applications and architectures and develop new applications that were previously challenging or impossible. It's still in its early days, and we believe that WebSocket will transform not only web development but also the way users can interact with information and devices over the Web.

■ ■ ■

Inspecting WebSocket Traffic

When experimenting and building applications with WebSockets, occasionally you may need to take a closer look at what exactly is happening under the covers. Throughout this book, we've used some of these tools to examine WebSocket traffic. In this appendix, we review three handy tools:

- Google Chrome Developer Tools: a set of HTML5 applications that ships with Chrome and allows you to inspect, debug, and optimize Web applications

- Google Chrome Network Internals (or "net-internals"): a set of tools that allows you to inspect network behavior including DNS lookups, SPDY, HTTP caching, as well as WebSocket

- Wireshark: a tool that enables you to analyze network protocol traffic

WebSocket Frame Inspection with Google Chrome Developer Tools

Google Chrome Developer Tools offer a wide range of features to help web developers. Here we focus on how it helps you learn about and debug WebSockets. If you're interested in learning more about Google Chrome Developer Tools in general, there's plenty of information available online.

To access the Developer Tools, open Google Chrome, then click the Customize and Control Google Chrome icon, located to the right of the address bar. Select **Tools ➤ Developer Tools**, as shown in Figure A-1. Most developers who use this tool frequently prefer the keyboard shortcut to the menu selection.

Figure A-1. *Opening Google Chrome Developer Tools*

Google Chrome Developer Tools provide you with detailed information about your page or application through eight panels, allowing you to perform the following tasks:

- Elements panel: inspect and modify the DOM tree

- Resources panel: inspect resources loaded

- Network panel: inspect network communication; this is the panel you'll use the most while building WebSocket-enabled applications.

- Sources panel: inspect source files and debug JavaScript

- Timeline panel: analyze where time is spent when loading or interacting with your page

- Profiles panel: profile the time and memory usage

- Audits panel: analyze the page as it loads and makes suggestions to improve it.

- Console: display error messages and execute commands. The console can be used along with any of the above panels. Press the Esc key on your keyboard to open and close the console. Along with the Network panel, the Console is the Web and WebSocket developer's best friend.

First, let's take a closer look at the Network panel. Open Chrome and navigate to http://www.websocket.org. We will use the Echo Test on websocket.org to learn about

the WebSocket Frame inspection that Google Chrome Developer Tools provide.
To access the Echo demo, click the Echo Test link on the page, which will take you to
`http://www.websocket.org/echo.html`. Open Google Chrome Developer Tools if you
haven't opened it yet, and click the Network panel. Make sure your Network panel is
empty. If it is not empty, click the Clean icon at the bottom of the Chrome Window, the
sixth icon from the left in Figure A-2.

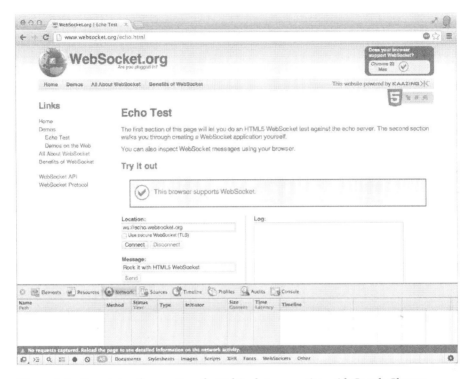

Figure A-2. *Examining the creation of a WebSocket connection with Google Chrome Developer Tools*

Notice that the location field contains a WebSocket URL that we'll connect to:
`ws://echo.websocket.org`. Click the Connect button to create the connection.
Notice that the WebSocket connection displays in your Network panel. Click the name,
`echo.websocket.org`, which is under the Headers tab; doing so allows you to look at the
WebSocket handshake (Figure A-3). Listing A-1 shows the entire WebSocket handshake.

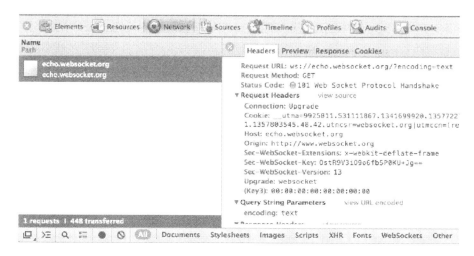

Figure A-3. *Inspecting the WebSocket handshake*

Listing A-1. The WebSocket Handshake

```
Request URL:ws://echo.websocket.org/?encoding=text
Request Method:GET
Status Code:101 Web Socket Protocol Handshake
```
Request Headers
```
Connection:Upgrade
Cookie:__utma=9925811.531111867.1341699920.1353720500.135372
5565.33; __utmb=9925811.4.10.1353725565; __utmc=9925811; __
utmz=9925811.1353725565.33.30.utmcsr=websocket.org|utmccn=(referral)|
utmcmd=referral|utmcct=/
Host:echo.websocket.org
Origin:http://www.websocket.org
Sec-WebSocket-Extensions:x-webkit-deflate-frame
Sec-WebSocket-Key:JfyxfhR8QIm3BSbOq/Tw5w==
Sec-WebSocket-Version:13
Upgrade:websocket
(Key3):00:00:00:00:00:00:00:00
```
Query String Parameters
```
encoding:text
```
Response Headers
```
Access-Control-Allow-Credentials:true
Access-Control-Allow-Headers:content-type
Access-Control-Allow-Origin:http://www.websocket.org
Connection:Upgrade
Date:Sat, 24 Nov 2012 03:08:27 GMT
Sec-WebSocket-Accept:Yr3WGnQMtPOktDVP1aBU3l5DfFI=
Server:Kaazing Gateway
Upgrade:WebSocket
(Challenge Response):00:00:00:00:00:00:00:00:00:00:00:00:00:00:00:00
```

Now, feel free to change the contents of the Message field and click the Send button. To inspect the WebSocket frames, you'll need to click on the Name on the far left again, which will refresh the panel on the right, adding the Frames tab, as shown in Figure A-4.

Figure A-4. *Inspecting WebSocket frames*

The WebSocket Frame inspector shows the data (which is text in this example), the length of the data, the time it was sent, as well as the direction of the data: a light green background indicates traffic from the browser to the WebSocket server (upload), and white indicates traffic from the server to the browser (download).

▓ **Note** As you're sending WebSocket messages, be sure to always click the Name column to trigger the refresh of the Frames tab.

As you navigate to the Sources tab, and locate the echo.js file, you see a variable called "websocket" that represents our WebSocket connection. By displaying the Console, you can simply send a message to the WebSocket server, using the send() function, as shown in Listing A-2.

Listing A-2. Sending a WebSocket Message Using the Chrome Console

```
websocket.send("Hello World!");
```

In Figure A-5 we sent a `Hello World!` message from the console, and you can see that in the Log window, the Echo service sent us a response. If you display your Network tab, you can also see the corresponding WebSocket frames.

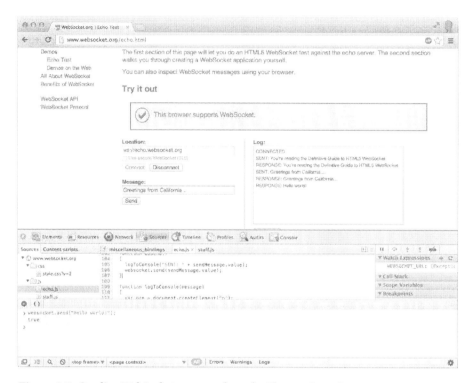

Figure A-5. *Sending WebSocket messages from the Chrome Console*

As demonstrated, the Chrome Developer Tools offer web developers a simple and effective way to "look under the hood" of their applications. Chrome's Network tab provides unique insight not only into the WebSocket handshake but also allows you to easily inspect the WebSocket frames.

Google Chrome Network Internals

Most of the time, Chrome Developer Tools display more than enough information to productively develop and debug web applications. Sometimes, however, lower-level details can help diagnose unusual connection failures or provide otherwise inaccessible information when investigating the behavior of the browser itself. Chrome has internal diagnostic pages that are extremely valuable in those rare situations in which you would like to observe the internal state of the browser. Chrome's internal tools expose events related to DNS requests, SPDY sessions, TCP timeouts, proxies, and other internal workings of the browser.

Google Chrome includes several additional utilities. For a list of them, type `chrome://about` in the browser's address bar.

▓ **Note** In Google Chrome, the URL `about:about` redirects to `chrome://about`. Other browsers, such as Mozilla Firefox, have useful URLs listed on their `about:about` pages.

The page displays the following list of useful internal Chrome utilities:

- `chrome://appcache-internals`
- `chrome://blob-internals`
- `chrome://bookmarks`
- `chrome://cache`
- `chrome://chrome-urls`
- `chrome://crashes`
- `chrome://credits`
- `chrome://dns`
- `chrome://downloads`
- `chrome://extensions`
- `chrome://flags`
- `chrome://flash`
- `chrome://gpu-internals`
- `chrome://history`
- `chrome://ipc`
- `chrome://inspect`
- `chrome://media-internals`
- `chrome://memory`
- `chrome://nacl`
- `chrome://net-internals`
- `chrome://view-http-cache`
- `chrome://newtab`

- chrome://omnibox
- chrome://plugins
- chrome://policy
- chrome://predictors
- chrome://profiler
- chrome://quota-internals
- chrome://settings
- chrome://stats
- chrome://sync-internals
- chrome://terms
- chrome://tracing
- chrome://version
- chrome://print

In the address bar, type chrome://net-internals. One use of net-internals is to inspect TCP socket events. These TCP sockets are used to transport WebSocket and other protocols used by the browser for communication. When you click Sockets on the left, Chrome displays the socket pools. What we're interested in is the currently active, live sockets, so click the View live sockets link. In a separate window or tab, open the WebSocket Echo test at http://www.websocket.org/echo.html, and click Connect. A new entry shows up right away, along with the following URL: ws://echo.websocket. org/?encoding=text. Click the entry, and on the right, you'll see the network internals, as shown in Listing A-4.

Listing A-4. Network Internals of a WebSocket Handshake

```
830: SOCKET
ws://echo.websocket.org/?encoding=text
Start Time: 2012-11-23 20:08:27.489

t=1353730107489 [st=  0] +SOCKET_ALIVE  [dt=?]
                          --> source_dependency = 828 (SOCKET_STREAM)
t=1353730107489 [st=  0]   +TCP_CONNECT  [dt=91]
                             --> address_list = ["174.129.224.73:80"]
t=1353730107489 [st=  0]     TCP_CONNECT_ATTEMPT  [dt=91]
                               --> address = "174.129.224.73:80"
t=1353730107580 [st= 91]   -TCP_CONNECT
                             --> source_address = "10.0.1.5:57878"
t=1353730107582 [st= 93]   SOCKET_BYTES_SENT
                             --> byte_count = 470
t=1353730107677 [st=188]   SOCKET_BYTES_RECEIVED
                             --> byte_count = 542
```

Now, from the window that displays `websocket.org`, let's send a message. The net-internals panel refreshes, and shows the number of bytes sent (see Figure A-6).

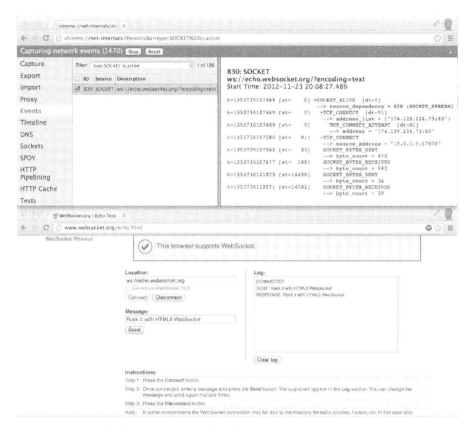

Figure A-6. *Google Chrome net-internals utility*

Much like the Google Developer Tools, net-internals is packaged and shipped with Google Chrome. Net-internals is a very handy tool if deeper, lower-level network diagnostics are required.

Analyzing Network Packets with Wireshark

Wireshark is a very powerful, free, and open source tool (available for download at `http://www.wireshark.org`) that provides detailed insight into network interfaces, allowing you to see and analyze what's traveling on the wire. Wireshark is a useful tool in WebSocket developers' hands but is widely used by network administrators, as well. Wireshark can capture live network data through the network interface that you can then export/import, filter, color code, and search.

Figure A-7 shows the Wireshark UI as it captures network packets. Under the menu bar and the main toolbar you see the Filter tool bar, which is used to filter the collected data. This data displays in a tabular format in the packet list pane. The packet details pane shows information about the packet selected in the packet list pane. The packet bytes pane, just above the status bar, displays the packet data, selected in the packet list pane.

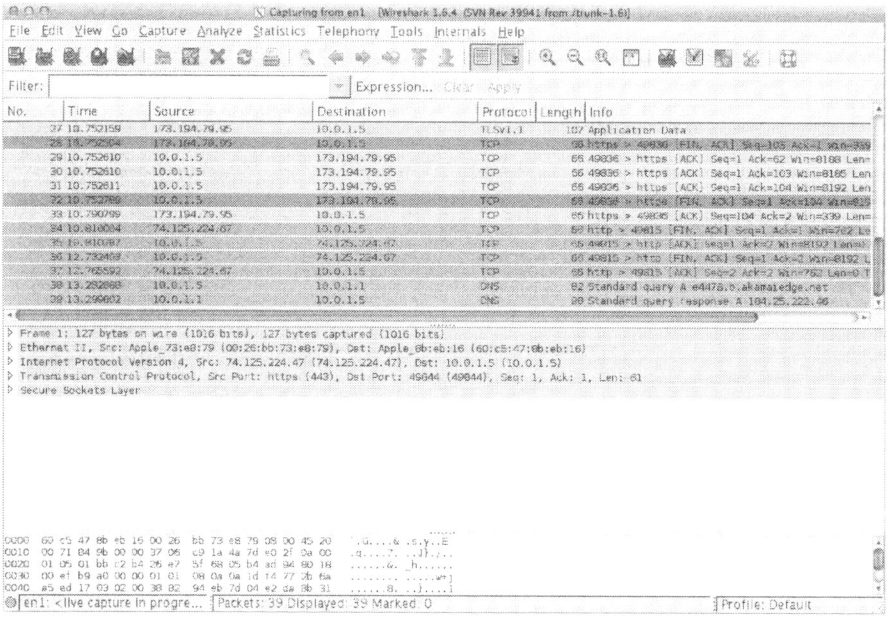

Figure A-7. *Wireshark capturing network packets*

Start Wireshark and select the network adapter you're using: if you're hard-wired to the network, your adapter will be different than when you use WiFi. In our experiment with Wireshark, we'll inspect the WebSocket traffic between a browser and a WebSocket server, running on websocket.org. To get started, navigate with your browser to http://www.websocket.org. Then, click the Echo Test link. You can alternatively point your browser directly at http://www.websocket.org/echo. Now, you're ready to establish a WebSocket connection. Click the Connect button.

Since there tends to be quite a bit of traffic on the network, the traffic between your browser and websocket.org quickly scrolls out of view. To ensure we see some useful data, we'll filter for traffic going to www.websocket.org.

Figure A-8 shows how you can filter out packets with a specific IP address: ip.dst_host==174.129.224.73. Wireshark supports the double-equal sign in the condition, as well as the eq operator. In this figure, also notice the WebSocket handshake in the packet details page.

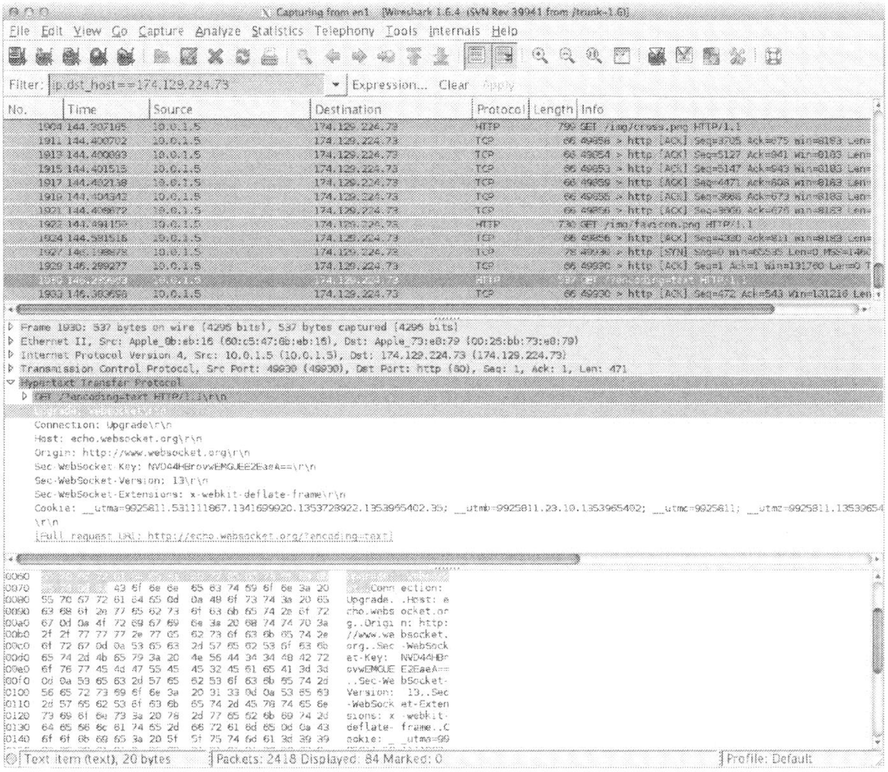

Figure A-8. *Filtering network packetsnetwork packets*

Another great feature of Wireshark is that it can follow various protocol streams. In Figure A-9 you can see how it follows a TCP stream. It displays the TCP segments that are on the same TCP connection as the selected packet. You can follow a protocol stream by right-mouse clicking on a packet in the packet list pane and choosing Follow from the context menu.

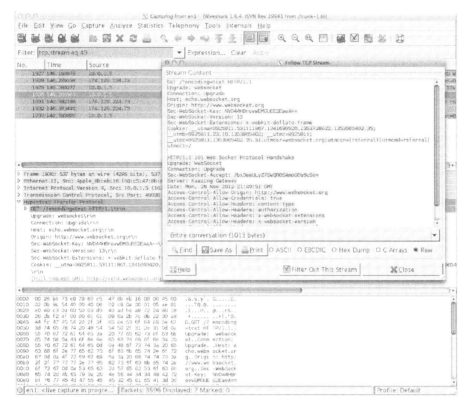

Figure A-9. *Following a TCP stream*

To see how Wireshark updates the packet list live, submit a WebSocket message in your browser. Figure A-10 shows how submitting the text, *Rock it with WebSocket*, to the Echo service appears in Wireshark.

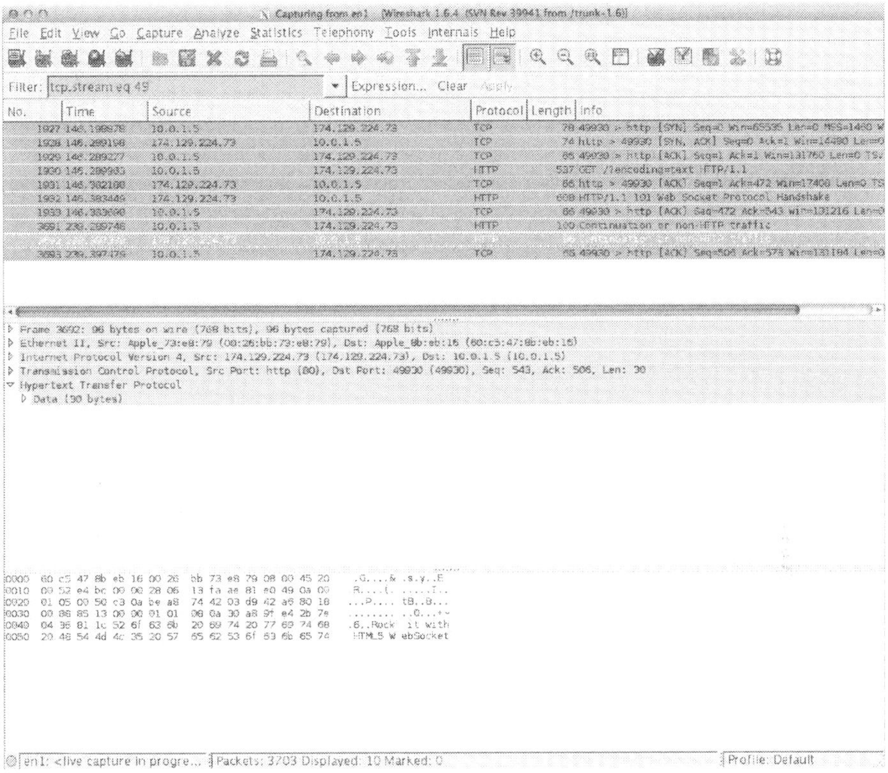

Figure A-10. *Wireshark updates live*

Summary

In this appendix, we explained some useful tools for inspecting, dissecting, and debugging WebSocket traffic. These tools will help you when building your WebSocket-enabled applications. The next appendix discusses the Virtual Machine (VM) we provide, which includes the open source code (libraries, tools, and servers) we used to build the examples in this book.

APPENDIX B

■ ■ ■

WebSocket Resources

Throughout this book, we've used a number of resources that help us build WebSocket applications every day. In this appendix, we walk through how to use the VM (virtual machine) that contains all the code and software pre-installed that you need to build or follow the examples in this book. We also summarize where to get all the libraries, servers, and other technologies we used in this book. Finally, we include a list of WebSocket servers and clients that are available at the time of writing this book.

Using the Virtual Machine

The VM accompanied by this book can be downloaded from the publisher's web site. Simply navigate to `http://apress.com` and search for this book's title (or go directly to `www.apress.com/9781430247401`). Click the Source Code/Downloads tab and click Download Now. After downloading it, you can start the VM using VirtualBox. VirtualBox is available as a free download from `http://virtualbox.org` for Windows, Mac, Linux, and Solaris host operating systems.

To open the VM, extract it, and double-click the `WebSocketBook.ova` file, or choose **File ➤ Import Appliance** from the menu of VirtualBox, and select the `WebSocketBook.vbox` file. The operating system of the VM is Ubuntu.

Once you've downloaded and installed the VM, you'll notice a few items on the desktop:

- Icons for Chapters 2–6

- A `README.txt` file

First, open and read the `README.txt`, which explains the servers and services that are automatically started for you when you install the VM. To build the examples described in Chapters 2–6, you can simply start building against the servers and libraries provided in the VM, which are described in the relevant chapter.

Tables B-1 and B-2 describe the servers and libraries that we use throughout the book and whether they are included in the VM.

Table B-1. *Servers Used in this Guide*

Server	Description	Where you can get it	Used in Chapters
Apache ActiveMQ	A popular open source message broker with support for messaging APIs and protocols, like JMS (Java Message Service) and STOMP (Simple or Streaming Text Oriented Messaging Protocol).	`http://activemq.apache.org`	5 and 7
node-xmpp-bosh	An open source server written by Dhruv Matani that enables XMPP connections over BOSH and WebSocket to any XMPP server. The server is implemented in JavaScript using Node.js.	`https://github.com/dhruvbird/node-xmpp-bosh`	4
Openfire	An open source RTC (real-time collaboration) server with support for XMPP (Extensible Messaging and Presence Protocol).	`http://www.igniterealtime.org/projects/openfire`	4
TightVNC	TightVNC is a cross-platform, open source VNC server.	`http://tightvnc.com`	**6**
`Websocket.org`	A publicly hosted WebSocket server with a simple Echo Service for testing and learning about WebSocket.	`http://www.websocket.org`	1, 3, and 7

Table B-2. *Libraries and Other Tools Used in this Guide*

Library/Tool	Description	Where you can get it	Used in Chapters
jQuery 1.8.2	A widely popular and commonly used open source JavaScript library simplifying cross-browser web development.	`http://jquery.com`	5
Node.js	A popular open source server for writing applications in JavaScript. Node.js is based on Google Chrome's performant open source V8 JavaScript with support for event-driven asynchronous I/O operations.	`http://nodejs.org`	3 and 6

(continued)

178

Table B-2. (*continued*)

Library/Tool	Description	Where you can get it	Used in Chapters
Node Package Manager (npm)	A Node.js package manager, allowing easy installation of Node.js packages.	http://npmjs.org	None (included in the VM)
Strophe.js	An open source XMPP library for JavaScript, originally created by Jeff Moffitt.	http://strophe.im/strophejs	4
VirtualBox	An open source virtualization product supporting Windows, Mac, Linux, and Solaris as the host operating system, and a significantly larger number of guest operating systems.	http://virtualbox.org	None (used to start the VM)

WebSocket Servers

While you can enable a server to accept WebSocket connections or indeed write your own WebSocket server, there are a few existing implementations that might make your life easier when developing your own WebSocket applications. At the time this book was written, the following are some of the WebSocket servers that are available (list provided by http://refcardz.dzone.com/refcardz/html5-websocket):

- Alchemy-Websockets (.NET): http://alchemywebsockets.net/

- Apache ActiveMQ: http://activemq.apache.org/

- apache-websocket (Apache module): https://github.com/disconnect/apache-websocket#readme

- APE Project (C): http://www.ape-project.org/

- Autobahn (virtual appliance): http://autobahn.ws/

- Caucho Resin (Java): http://www.caucho.com/

- Cowboy: https://github.com/extend/cowboy

- Cramp (Ruby): http://cramp.in/

- Diffusion (Commercial product): http://www.pushtechnology.com/home

- EM-WebSocket (Ruby): https://github.com/igrigorik/em-websocket

- Extendible WebSocket Server (PHP): https://github.com/wkjagt/Extendible-Web-Socket-Server

- gevent-websocket (Python): `http://www.gelens.org/code/gevent-websocket/`

- GlassFish (Java): `http://glassfish.java.net/`

- Goliath (Ruby): `https://github.com/postrank-labs/goliath`

- Jetty (Java): `http://jetty.codehaus.org/jetty/`

- jWebsocket (Java): `http://jwebsocket.org/`

- Kaazing WebSocket Gateway (Commercial product): `http://kaazing.com/`

- libwebsockets (C): `http://git.warmcat.com/cgi-bin/cgit/libwebsockets/`

- Misultin (Erlang): `https://github.com/ostinelli/misultin`

- net.websocket (Go): `http://code.google.com/p/go.net/websocket`

- Netty (Java): `http://netty.io/`

- Nugget (.NET): `http://nugget.codeplex.com/`

- phpdaemon (PHP): `http://phpdaemon.net/`

- Pusher (cloud service): `http://pusher.com/`

- pywebsockets (Python): `http://code.google.com/p/pywebsocket/`

- RabbitMQ (Erlang): `https://github.com/videlalvaro/rabbitmq-websockets`

- Socket.io (Node.js): `http://socket.io/`

- SockJS-node (Node): `https://github.com/sockjs/sockjs-node`

- SuperWebSocket (.NET): `http://superwebsocket.codeplex.com/`

- Tomcat (Java): `http://tomcat.apache.org/`

- Tornado (python): `http://www.tornadoweb.org/`

- txWebSocket (Python/Twisted): `https://github.com/rlotun/txWebSocket`

- vert.x (Java): `http://vertx.io/`

- Watersprout (PHP): `https://github.com/chrisnetonline/WaterSpout-Server/blob/master/server.php`

- web-socket-ruby (Ruby): `https://github.com/gimite/web-socket-ruby`

- Webbit (Java): `https://github.com/webbit/webbit`

- WebSocket-Node (Node.js): `https://github.com/Worlize/WebSocket-Node`

- websockify (Python): `https://github.com/kanaka/websockify`

- XSockets (.NET): `http://xsockets.net/`

- Yaws (Erlang)`http://yaws.hyber.org/websockets.yaws`

Index